Thread of Hope

Thread of Hope

MEDITATIONS FOR WOMEN

Faye Hill Thompson

1	2	3	4	5	6	7	8	9	10
00	09	08	07	06	05	04	03	02	01

*To my mother, father,
husband, and daughter,
who taught me God is always present,
threading His hope into my life.*

Table of Contents

Acknowledgments

"Oh, Lord, my God ... How great Thou art" for conceiving, birthing, implementing, and fulfilling this vision You put in me, moving me past anger, denial, grief, and fear to write what was on my heart.

Thanks to:

Mom and Dad. I wish everyone could know such unconditional love. Thanks for perusing every devotional story, offering your parental guidance, prayers, and support.

Sister Ann, Brother Paul, and their families. For allowing me to share family memories; giving me time, space, and freedom in which to do this; and for your prayers, I give you my heartfelt thanks.

Friends Rhonda, Eleanor K., Eleanor Y., Fran, Linda, Steve, and Char, my prayer warriors. Your constant prayers are the core of this book. How blessed I am to have you as friends. Rhonda, for the time you took from your busy schedule to read and critique my devotions, I'm grateful beyond words.

Dawn, Jane, Peggy, and the Concordia Publishing House staff. You believed in this project from its onset. You walk the talk. Your faith, prayers, understanding, and professionalism are deeply appreciated.

Pastor Ted Schroeder and Dr. Roger Palms, for passing on your writing craft through your classes.

Ilene and Jim, for assisting me in the computer lab. Ilene, thanks for your patience with me in class while I learned how to run a computer.

Pastors Harvey, David and Cheryl, and Mike, for giving The Word flesh, allowing me to learn from your theological and practical knowledge.

Fran, for being my mentor and friend.

Teresa, friend and cheerleader, for helping type my earlier manuscripts and teaching me to believe in my dream and to be myself.

Barb, for encouraging me, when my spirit ebbed, with your cards and sayings and for sharing with me the books from your classes on how to be a creative writer.

My friends. You've been a part of my life, of my growing and emerging. May God's love forever surround you.

Daughter, Melia, and husband, Noel. You've patiently supported me as I've altered our family life to devote time and energy to this amazing project.

Melia, what a gift God gave when He chose me to be your mother. Special thanks for sharing the computer, making cheat sheets for your "technophobic" mother, and for formatting my final manuscript.

Noel, I always wondered why God brought two English majors together! Thank you, more than I can say, for editing my endless devotional stories, pointing out possibilities rather than problems; for sharing with me your insights, prayers, patience, and love.

And to you, the reader. I've prayed for you in every thought I've shared. May you find yourself loved by Christ, as I have found, even in the hurdles.

Introduction

You're about to embark on a journey recounting many hurdles. These hurdles are situations we, as women, sooner or later encounter—though a few are unique to me. You'll discover hurdles as ordinary as first love, wanting a perfect husband, sending a kindergartner off to the first day of school, giving a teenager wings, being frustrated by everyday routine, and finding purpose in life when old. You'll find some hurdles filled with heartache: miscarriage, unfulfilled dreams, and losing a loved one. A few hurdles are unexplainable, such as an amazing story about a late-night rescue and the awesome power of nature.

These devotional stories came from my journalings. Had I not written my thoughts down, as scattered and incongruent as they were, it would have been more difficult to see, years later, the thread of hope Christ weaves in my life. Care to journal as we go along? After every devotional story and prayer, I've included a section called "Journal Jottings" to help guide your thoughts. Whether you choose to journal, I encourage you to think about the question and how it applies to your situation.

As you live through these hurdles with me, you'll experience the endless emotions of life—from its laughter and joy to its seriousness and sadness. I don't consider any of these stories I've written to be heroic, just glimpses of how a loving God teaches me every day how to see His thread of hope in every situation. And each day I see anew how God is at work in my life through Word and Sacrament, changing and renewing me as His child.

These inspirational stories have been written from my scape. As with any writer who uses real-life stories, I've struggled to tell them accurately, not wanting to hurt or misrepresent anyone, particularly my family and friends. There is no right way to read this book. You may choose to read it through in its entirety to catch the way God weaves His thread of hope throughout life. Or you might want to read those inspirational stories that apply to your life now, keeping the others for the journey ahead. I like to think of this book as one you'll grow with as your life moves through its seasons. Mother, daughter, sister, grandmother, or granddaughter, come, celebrate with me what it means to be a woman of hope despite our hurdles.

The hurdles I've written about are in a loose, chronological order. I hope that will keep our journey all the more interesting. Life, you see, is sometimes like that, loosely woven, not easily understood. It has been for me anyway. But I know that God is in my life. Don't listen for my words; listen for His. You're not sure what the thread of hope in these hurdles is all about? Well, come along. We'll discover it together.

Faye Hill Thompson

The Ugly Bird

OVERCOMING AN UGLY, HOPELESS IMAGE

Now after He rose early on the first day
of the week, He appeared first to Mary
Magdalene, from whom He had cast out
seven demons. Mark 16:9 NRSV

"I can't go on with my life," I told my mother over the phone. "It has no meaning. I see no reason for living."

My mother told me she would come over immediately. I could hear the urgency in her voice.

As my mother hung up the phone, she already knew from past conversations how depressed I felt. She realized how I'd planned to go back to teaching after having raised my daughter to early childhood. Now she sensed, along with me, that this was nearly impossible, though the timing was right. I simply didn't have the physical strength necessary to resume teaching. We both knew it.

When my mother arrived, I expected the usual lecture about looking on the bright side of life and refusing to dwell on the negative. Instead, Mom quietly asked if I'd sit with her on the sofa.

As we sat down, Mom pointed to the picture, "The Ugly Bird," painted by my favorite artist, which hung on my living room wall. She asked me to explain whom I saw in this picture and to tell her what this figure was doing. I told her I saw a formless figure holding a fragile, scraggly bird.

I asked Mom the same question she'd asked me. Mom explained her interpretation. She told me she saw a person who mirrored deep faith. As she moved closer to the picture, she named Him. Jesus. He was the one holding this scraggly, fragile bird in His arms.

Holding me in her arms, Mom concluded her thoughts. "I think you see yourself as this ugly, hopeless bird. You need someone to hold you. I will hold you as long as I am able. Jesus, however, will hold you forever, just like He does in the picture."

Someday I wouldn't see myself as ugly and hopeless. Christ would change that, Mom reassured me. She held me for a long time, then quietly left.

Alone, I remembered a woman in the Scriptures who probably thought she was ugly and hopeless too when Jesus met her. Maybe she even had emotional problems like mine. But Jesus granted her emotional healing just as He would grant her salvation. He cast out seven demons. Her name was Mary Magdalene (Mark 16:9).

If Jesus could restore a woman such as Mary Magdalene to wholeness, He could do the same for me. Just as Jesus helped Mary Magdalene see herself differently, He'd certainly do the same for me. Wouldn't He?

Although Jesus healed Mary Magdalene immediately, I imagine it took many experiences and lessons at Jesus' side before she, through His power, became the confident, hopeful woman who later announced Jesus' resurrection.

I wonder what kind of experiences I'll go through and which lessons I'll learn at His side as Jesus changes me into the hopeful, confident woman He intends me to be. As Jesus helps me become this woman, I will be renewed in my Baptism and led to His arms of forgiveness with new meaning or purpose in my life.

Prayer

Lord God, because of my sin, I look ugly and hopeless. But You have changed my condition through the death and resurrection of Jesus. Thank You for Your plan of salvation. Thank You for offering me forgiveness through Jesus Christ. Give me strength to confess my sins, grace to receive Your forgiveness, and renewed assurance in Jesus as my Lord and Savior. Thank You for restoring me to wholeness through Your Word and Sacrament, and for working in me to make me into the hopeful person You intend me to be. In Jesus' name. Amen.

Journal Jottings

Share in your journal about a time in your life when you felt ugly and hopeless. How did Christ restore your hope? Note: To understand the "ugly bird" period of my life, it's helpful to glimpse my earlier years.

Sweetie Pie

CREATING A FEELING OF SPECIALNESS

"Many women do noble things,
but you surpass them all."
Proverbs 31:29

I awoke that morning, after the spring rains had melted the winter snow, with one thought racing through my mind, "Will anyone remember I'm turning 8 years old today?"

While eating my hot oatmeal with my brother and sister, the phone rang. To my surprise, it was for me. Excitedly, I answered, "Hello."

"This is Sweetie Pie." I immediately recognized the voice. Her real name was Mabel. All her friends, however, affectionately called her Sweetie Pie. Sweetie Pie was head cook in the cafeteria at my school. She and I had become friends because my leg brace prevented me from spending noon recess outside. Instead, I sat in the cafeteria with her as she scrubbed lunch trays.

"Happy Birthday, Faye," Sweetie Pie chirped. "I rose early this morning and baked something special for you." It was hard for me to hold back my excitement. "Could you come to my home with your mother before school to pick up your surprise?"

"Oh, sure," I promised as I hurriedly thanked her and hung up the phone.

In less than five minutes, Mom and I had whipped on our coats and were dodging mud puddles up Sweetie Pie's long lane. Pausing to give Sweetie Pie a gigantic hug and scrape the mud off my shoes, I entered her farm home.

There, sitting on her massive oak dining room table, was the prettiest cake I'd ever seen. With a doll in the center, the cake was shaped like a huge pink-frosted petticoat. On the dolly's petticoat, inscribed in a deeper rose frosting, were the words, "Happy Birthday, Faye." Light pink roses edged the dolly's petticoat.

I stood speechless for the longest time, admiring the masterpiece. After giving Sweetie Pie another hug, I asked my mom if I could take the cake to school with me. She persuaded me to let her take the cake home instead. On the way to school, I asked my mom how Sweetie Pie knew it was my birthday. She had no idea.

Before the first bell rang, I quizzed my girlfriends if they knew how Sweetie Pie had found out it was my birthday. No one had a clue. At noon, as I passed through the cafeteria line, I felt like queen-for-a-day as I told the kids around me about the special cake Sweetie Pie had baked for me.

While watching Sweetie Pie cleaning up after lunch that day, I solved the puzzle of how she knew this was my birthday. Of all things—I had told her. While jabbering with her one day, I remembered letting it slip out that my birthday was coming up. Bless her, even with her busy routine, Sweetie Pie had remembered and made me feel so special on my birthday.

Although she's long since gone to heaven, whenever I see a birthday cake in my honor, I think of Sweetie Pie. She was a compassionate woman of the noblest kind, sent from God, who baked for me far more than a birthday cake. This God-fearing woman shared her response to God's goodness with others, making them feel so special despite her busyness. And baked inside of me was a desire to do the same. Bless you, Sweetie Pie, for remembering me.

Prayer

Bake within my life, Lord, a desire to make others feel special on a birthday or other special day. Especially those who may face challenges or have difficulties. Show me how I can serve You by serving them and sharing with them the hope, strength, and love that comes only from knowing You and the promise of salvation through faith in Jesus Christ. In Jesus' name. Amen.

Journal Jottings

How can you show a little girl who needs to be remembered that she is special?

Mammoth Hills

PERSEVERING, EVEN WHEN DREAMS STAND STILL

"The battle is the LORD's."
1 Samuel 17:47

When I was a little girl, my mother would read to me before she turned out the lights at bedtime. My favorite children's book was *The Little Engine That Could*. In this story, everything is going smoothly until the engine and its railroad cars arrive at a mammoth hill. Suddenly, the little engine pulls back, wondering how it will ever pull this many railroad cars up the hill. Although it seems impossible, the little engine won't give up. It perseveres. Repeating the words, "I think I can," it finally pulls its railroad cars up the hill. I would remember this story time and again, as I struggled up the mammoth hills of my life.

One such hill came the spring of my fourth-grade year. For my birthday, my parents bought me a shiny, new bicycle complete with training wheels. I had wanted this bicycle for months. As my eyes danced over its frame, I dreamed someday, although I wore a leg brace, I'd ride that bicycle alone.

My parents worked diligently with me. The days of training drew into weeks. I had no trouble getting my left leg to push the pedal down. The problem came when I tried to make my right leg follow suit. I just didn't have enough muscle power. Without the ability to alternately push both pedals, I couldn't begin to get my bike to move. After weeks of trying unsuccessfully, I figured there was no use. I'd never be able to ride a bike alone. Despondently, I placed my bike in the garage, intending to never ride it again.

That night, thinking of my unfulfilled dream, I remembered a youth in the Bible who had faced an impossible task. When the Palestinian champion Goliath challenged the Israelites to a fight, all they wanted to do was retreat—all except for the shepherd youth David. With his slingshot and five small stones, clothed in trust in God and armed with the name of God, David stepped forward to fight the giant Goliath in battle.

God authored the possible to emerge from the impossible. With one mere stone, David killed Goliath. The battle and the victory belonged to the God of the Israelites. (1 Samuel 17:20–54).

Under my bed covers I pondered, David didn't think of retreating when everything seemed to be against him, when his goal and the goal of all Israel looked to be impossible. Why should I retreat when my goal of riding a bike appears to be the same? God had authored the possible to come out of the impossible for David and Israel. Could He do the same for me? Following David's example, I would pray, trust, and not give up.

After school the next afternoon, I pulled my bike out of the garage. As I did, Mom mentioned, "Your dad and I have been talking. If I strap your right leg to the pedal so it can't move, then occasionally give your bike a push from behind, do you think you could ride your bike by yourself?" What did I have to lose?

It worked! God, working through my parents, had helped me make it up one mammoth hill to overcome a giant. This was only one of many steep hills He'd helped me climb.

Another gigantic hill faced me the summer after I'd graduated from college. Whenever I saw a teaching position advertised in the newspaper for which I was qualified, I'd send a letter of inquiry. After sending more than 100 letters,

I hadn't received a nibble. With only two weeks until a new school year started, I wanted to give up my dream of becoming a teacher. No school system was going to hire a handicapped teacher fresh out of college with no teaching experience.

As I glumly viewed the growing list of schools that hadn't responded, the story of David and Goliath resurfaced. Rather than retreating when my goal seemed unachievable, I could look to God, trusting Him to author the possible from the impossible.

The next morning, I saw a new teaching position advertised. This private school needed a secondary language arts and social studies teacher immediately. After reviewing my credentials and interviewing me, Sister Janita hired me. With God authoring the possible, He'd helped me make it over another gigantic hill.

Daily I rejoice that I have a heavenly Father who sent His Son to overcome the most impossible hill of all—sin, death, and the power of the devil. Only He can make the impossible possible.

Prayer

When hills look too monstrous to climb, when goals look unachievable, walk with me, Lord. Send Your Holy Spirit to increase my faith and trust in You. Even as You have sent Jesus to conquer the giants of sin and the grave, You have promised to strengthen me for the giants and hills I face daily. In the name of Jesus Christ, who gives me strength. Amen.

Journal Jottings

Do you have a goal that seems impossible? How is God helping you move forward?

Blue Skort

If one falls down,
his friend can help him up.
Ecclesiastes 4:10

I was scared when I awoke that summer morning between my fifth- and sixth-grade school year. I faced a painful, unpleasant surgery the next day. For weeks, I'd had nightmares because of the ordeal that lay ahead. On this particular morning, those frightening visions were even worse. As horrifying images of dripping IVs, razor-sharp knives, and oversized operating tables rushed through my mind, my nervousness and anxiety increased. "How will I keep from going crazy this last day before surgery?" I questioned aloud.

After getting dressed, I trudged downstairs. While choking down a bowl of cereal, hypnotized by my thoughts, the phone rang. Mom answered it and passed the phone to me.

"Can you come over and play with me today?" my cousin Eunice asked in her usual bubbly voice. I replied with a hesitant yes.

Eunie (her nickname) and her mother picked me up. When we arrived at her place, Eunie asked her mom to drop us off by her playhouse. She knew how fond I was of this place her dad had built for her.

Stacking cement blocks on top of one another, Eunie's dad had formed the frame of her playhouse. By placing additional cement blocks, zigzagging them in and out, he'd developed an elaborate floor plan inside, including a kitchen, living/dining room, bedroom, and bath. Eunie's mom had furnished it with an old table and chairs, several worn rugs, and some used dishes and utensils.

Knowing how much I liked tea parties, Eunie and I set the table for four: two for our dolls and two for us. After pouring the Kool-Aid and placing a cookie on each plate, we pulled our dolls up to the table.

Midway through our tea party, noticing how sad I was, Eunie inquired, "Fazie (my nickname), what's wrong with you today?"

After listening as I poured out my fears, she scolded me slightly, "Don't worry so much. I'm sure your surgery will go much better than you think." Realizing I'd be in a full-length leg cast for six weeks while recuperating, she added with a bounce in her voice, "Besides, I'll come visit you a lot while you're getting better." My spirits started to lift.

We brought our dolls to the "real house" to take a nap, and ate a scrumptious lunch. Then we headed to the corn crib. Eunie stacked one hay bale on top of another to create makeshift steps. I followed her up the steps to the top of the crib where we could see the whole farmstead. Using an old piece of tin as a microphone, we pretended we were auditioning for Hollywood.

Then we put on our bathing suits and hitched a ride on the hay wagon to the creek. There, we slid down the creek's bank and floated downstream on a gigantic tractor tire inner tube. More than once, the inner tube tipped over, making us giggle all the more. We laughed all the way home. When Eunie's mom saw us, she marched us straight to the tub.

As the grandfather clock chimed six, it was time for me to go home. Except for the brief conversation that morning, Eunie hadn't mentioned my surgery the rest of the day. Neither had I.

Just before heading home, my cousin handed me a present. Unwrapping it, I found a pretty blue skort with a white, ruffled crop top that she'd picked out herself.

Hugging me, Eunie said, "Fazie, I'll think about you every night when I say my prayers."

Squeezing her tightly, with tears in my eyes, I whispered, "Thanks, Eunie, for everything. I couldn't have had more fun. You took my mind off my surgery and helped me feel a whole lot better."

She chirped, "Isn't that what best friends are for?"

I went to bed that night thanking God for knowing my every need and providing a fun-filled day. I sensed this day, with all its frivolous memories, would carry me through darker days ahead.

That blue skort still hangs in my closet along with my memories.

Prayer

Heavenly Father, when a friend is facing an unpleasant ordeal, help me to be there for her and remind her that Jesus is always with her. Teach me to listen to her concerns, offer to pray, and share encouragement to soothe her troubled spirit. As Jesus pointed His disciples to You and Your promises, help me to share the reality of Your saving love in Christ and Your promise to work in all things for our good. In Jesus' compassionate name, I pray. Amen.

Journal Jottings

What activities have you encouraged a friend to do to help them momentarily think of something else, rather than a trying experience ahead of them?

Signed,
Your Secret Admirers

GIVING WITHOUT PRAISE OR RECOGNITION

"Then your Father, who sees what is
done in secret, will reward you."
Matthew 6:4

Can you remember when you were given a gift with no
name attached? I recall this happening to me twice.

The first time occurred the summer I'd had surgery on
my leg. For six days in a row, I received a card. Each was
signed the same, *Your Secret Pal.* I had fun guessing who
that secret pal might be.

On the seventh day, the envelope was bigger than the
others I'd received. I guessed this must be my last one, and
I hurriedly opened it, certain I'd solve the mystery. To my
dismay, it was signed in the same manner. I scrutinized the
card and envelope for a clue. I found none.

A similar event happened the night I graduated from
high school. In front of my graduating class, the school
board president asked me to come to the stage. To my surprise, he handed me a plain white envelope. On the outside were typed four words: *Faye Hill, Determination
Award.* A monetary gift was tucked inside a blank sheet of
paper. There were no signature or clues.

To this day, I don't know who gave me those gifts. Why
didn't the person sign his or her name? I wouldn't come to
understand this until years later when our daughter was a
freshman in high school.

During her first year, Melia was struggling with friendships. On Valentine's Day, my husband and I ordered a balloon bouquet and had it delivered to her at school. We didn't see the surprise in her eyes, the smile on her lips, or the dimples in her cheeks when she received it. Neither did we see her puzzled look when she read the card, which was signed, *Your Secret Admirers.* But we imagined the joy in her heart, and our spirits were lifted too.

I remember how I couldn't wait until our daughter came home from school, balancing her balloon bouquet, full of guesses as to who had sent it. She never found out (until now). But she will always remember the love she felt when she received that secret gift.

As Christians, we can always remember another gift given in love. This gift, however, was not secret or anonymous, but was announced by an angel choir. The gift was our Savior, Jesus Christ, who died for our sins and rose on Easter that we may all have eternal life with Him.

Although I couldn't imagine a reason at the time, I now know why those people sent those secret gifts all those years ago. I also know why we sent the balloon bouquet to our daughter. And I know why God sent Jesus: love.

Prayer

Lord and Giver of all good things, help me to use every opportunity to share the gift of Your love. Encourage me in the joy of performing secret kindnesses for others. And remind me that I love others because Jesus first loved me. In His name I pray. Amen.

Journal Jottings

Describe a secret act of kindness for someone that will lift their spirits and point them to Jesus—the greatest gift.

Roller-Skating Party
TEMPTATION TO SIT ON THE SIDELINES

Encourage the faint-hearted,
help the weak, be patient with them all.
1 Thessalonians 5:14 RSV

My parents had encouraged me to attend my eighth-grade class roller-skating party. I objected out of fear that I would be left timidly sitting alone on the bleachers while my classmates spun merrily past me. The only excitement I could envision was wishing I could skate with them. Still protesting, my parents dropped me off at the rink.

After my classmates had been fitted with skates and were wildly racing past me on the bleachers, the manager approached and cheerfully asked why I wasn't skating with the rest of my group. I pointed to my leg brace, embarrassed over the attention.

"Why, we're not going to let that stop you from having a good time," he replied in an enthusiastic tone. "You find a couple of friends to help you pick out the right size skates. I'll be right back."

When two friends skated by, I flagged them over and asked for their assistance. In minutes, they had me fitted with skates.

The manager returned with his assistant. Gently but firmly they lifted me and held on to my arms, one on each side, while I became accustomed to the wheels on my feet. "I just know I'm not going to be able to skate" I said, my voice quivering. "Why should I even try?"

They paid little attention to my fears but resolutely moved me onto the rink.

The steps I took were not fancy or fast, but with each move I accomplished without falling, I gained confidence. To my surprise, before long I'd skated successfully around the entire rink, thanks to my partners. Even more surprising to me, my classmates joined us for short intervals. By the end of the night, the three of us had become the life of the party.

For our skating finale, the manager picked me up, and before I knew what was happening, spun several figure eights with me. Then, as I unlaced my skates, he whispered, "You see? You don't have to sit on the sidelines. You can become involved too. It just takes a little more fortitude and creativity."

I grinned broadly. "And a willingness to try," I added.

As I grew up, I would come to understand how good those words were for all aspects of life. And I added one more word: faith. Faith as a baptized child of God. Faith to grab hold of Jesus as He reaches out to me. Faith that follows where Jesus leads. Faith that Jesus is the source of my strength and my salvation.

Prayer

Lord Jesus, help me not to allow situations to keep me on life's bleachers. Remind me that just as You made it possible for Peter to overcome his lack of faith and come to You by walking on water, dear Jesus, that through You, all things are possible. In Your name I pray. Amen.

Journal Jottings

When has a hesitant spirit stopped you from doing something you really wanted to do?

Grammy's Surprise

I thank my God every time
I remember you. Philippians 1:3

I loved my grandpa dearly. Dressed in bib overalls, he'd often drive his blue Chevy to the farm after I got home from school and ask if I'd like to run an errand with him. I always did because then I'd get to stay overnight with Grammy and him. That was a real treat. Throughout my elementary years, Grandpa and I went on many excursions and became best buddies. But like all good seasons, this one was cut short.

When I was 12, Grandpa suffered a severe heart attack and died. Life just didn't seem the same without him. I didn't enjoy going to my grandmother's house nearly as much because everything reminded me of him.

I loved my grandmother, but not in the same way as I had Grandpa. Yet I always knew, with her resilient spirit and indomitable faith in God, she had my best interests at heart. She wanted me to grow up to lead a Christ-filled life.

My grandmother lived several years after my grandfather died. Two months before Grammy died, when she sensed her days on earth were numbered, she made a simple request. She wanted to visit individually with each of her grandchildren. I came home one weekend during my sophomore year in college to take my turn. I remember how scared I was. I shivered at the thought of seeing Grammy in her bed, dying.

That morning, my grammy comforted me. She told stories she wanted me to remember about her life. She listened while I shared concerns regarding mine. And she talked freely and without fear about death. Before I left, she shared two passages from Scripture that God had used repeatedly to strengthen her faith.

The first passage, from Psalm 23, assured her that God, as our shepherd, takes care of everything we need. He assuredly brings us to dwell with Him forever. The second passage, taken from Philippians 4:4–7, reminded her to rejoice, pray, and give thanks, no matter the circumstance because the Lord's hand is in everything.

We joined hands in prayer. With tears and a tight hug, we shared with each other a long blessing. I no longer feared having Grammy leave me. God had used her to prepare me.

After my grandmother's funeral several weeks later, my mother and father drove me to the airport so I could catch a plane to join my concert choir group on spring tour. Knowing that her possessions would soon be distributed to her family, I told my dad, "I sure hope Grammy didn't forget me." Dad remained silent, alone with his thoughts.

Two months later, I received my junior college degree. After I'd opened what I thought were all my gifts, Dad handed me one more. By the tender way in which he presented it, I knew it was something very precious. Nestled in a small, white satin-covered box, lay Grammy's gift to me, her wedding ring.

Choked with emotion, Dad whispered, "I guess your grandmother didn't forget you."

When I gaze at that ring today, a symbol of so many precious memories, I am filled with thankfulness to God. I remember my grandparents and the deep, special love they demonstrated. I'm ashamed, though, at how I worried if my grandmother had left me a tangible gift. While she lived, she'd already given me a far greater, intangible gift—a legacy of a rebounding spirit and unwavering faith in God.

Prayer

Forgive me, Lord God, when I worry about tangible things, and remind me it's the intangible gifts that count the most. Gifts such as parents and grandparents who love me. Gifts such as the resilient spirit and faith You gave my grandmother and nurtured through Your Word and Sacrament—a saving faith in the most wonderful gift, Jesus our Savior. In Jesus' name I pray. Amen.

Journal Jottings

Describe a time you worried about a tangible gift but learned that intangible gifts are more precious.

Valentine Cookie Bake

COMBATING LONELINESS

*The LORD is close to the brokenhearted
and saves those who are crushed in spirit.*
Psalm 34:18

It was a frigid February morning. I was a junior in college. A transfer student, I'd been on the campus only a few months. My roommate was out with friends she'd known since her freshman year. The girls on my floor that I usually chummed around with had gone home for the weekend. Because of subzero temperatures and a long drive home, my parents had advised me to stay on campus. Alone in my dorm room, I was having quite the pity party.

Before heading down to the laundry room to tackle my dirty clothes, I plopped down on my bed to pray. In my prayer, I asked God to take away my loneliness. God did more than that.

With a hurting, lonely heart, I studied as my clothes swished in the machine. I thought if I could just get involved in my class assignments, then I might forget how lonely I felt. As the washer droned, however, the ache in my heart only intensified.

As I waited for my clothes to finish, a dorm mate filled the washing machine next to mine and skipped over to the desk where I was studying. "You look like you've lost your last friend," she commented.

Between the assignments and not going home for the weekend, I told her I felt like I had.

"Yeah, with all the gals I usually bum around with gone for the weekend, I feel a little like you. It won't do either of us any good, though, if all we do is mope around and tell each other how bad we feel."

Pausing, she continued. "I have a great idea to perk us up. While our clothes are tumbling in the machines, let's have a valentine cookie bake."

I offered all kinds of excuses, ranging from my need to study to the reality of not having the necessary ingredients on hand in our ill-equipped dorm kitchen. She would hear none of these. She looked at me with spirited eyes and said, "I'll be back in a jiff."

Approximately half an hour later, she returned with a sack full of groceries from a store close to campus. On top, I spotted a recipe for sugar cookies and several heart-shaped cookie cutters. Catching my inquisitiveness, she told me she'd brought them back with her after Christmas break.

Finding two aprons, some make-do utensils, and a couple of cookie sheets in the dorm's kitchen, we started baking. By the time we'd mixed, kneaded, and cut the dough into various-sized hearts, I don't recall who had more flour on them—the cookies or us. I also can't remember who laughed harder or popped more fresh cookies into her mouth. I do recollect, though, that the loneliness and bro-kenheartedness we'd both been experiencing subsided.

That night, as I turned off the light, I pondered how differently this friend and I had handled our loneliness. Instead of feeling sorry for herself and waiting for God to take away her lonelies like I had, she was motivated to interact with someone else. I'm thankful that I was the blessed recipient of her action. Beginning with the camaraderie we'd experienced while baking, we became best of friends our remaining college years.

In the years since, I've come to realize that we were all lonely in our sin until God sent Jesus to be our best friend.

The gift of faith in Jesus and the forgiveness and eternal life we receive because of His death and resurrection motivate us to share love with those around us—especially those who are lonely.

Now, isn't that quite a recipe for combating loneliness?

Prayer

Gracious Lord, remind me that I don't have to wait for someone to come along and take away my loneliness because You have already sent that Someone. Motivate me, through Your Holy Spirit, to find others with whom I can interact. Make me aware of ways I can witness to Your faithfulness to me. In Jesus' name I pray. Amen.

Journal Jottings

Write a recipe for overcoming loneliness.

Summer Weekends with the Flaathens

SAYING GOOD-BYE

*And I am sure that He who began a
good work in you will bring it to
completion at the day of Jesus Christ.*
Philippians 1:6 RSV

During the summer between my junior and senior years of college, I went to study at the university in Oslo, Norway. Groggily de-boarding my transatlantic flight, I met the Flaathens: Alf, IngaMae, and Elisabeth. Their daughter Toni and I had become friends at college.

I spent my first few days with the Flaathens in their spacious, beautifully decorated home, becoming acquainted with the country, its people, and its traditions.

Elisabeth, Toni's younger sister, invited me to go to the market one day.

Lightheartedly walking from one shop to the other, we gathered the foodstuffs her mother needed for the weekend: fresh cod at the meat shop, milk and cheese at the cheese shop, a loaf of freshly baked bread at the bakery. On our way home, we stopped at the produce stand to buy some homegrown fruits and vegetables, then at an outside market to pick out a bouquet of fresh flowers.

Because of the Flaathen's gracious hospitality and genuine Christian fellowship, I felt a special kinship with them and an appreciation for their homeland.

Every Friday afternoon after class, Alf would pick me up in his car. On the drive home, he'd ask how I wanted to spend the weekend. In the course of time, the Flaathens showed me the sights of their beloved city: the intricately-detailed Vigeland Sculptures in Frogner Park, the changing of the guard at the Royal Palace, the Viking Ships House, famous for its three excavated Viking ships, and much more.

One weekend, we meandered by boat through the Oslo Fjord. I captured breathtaking photos of pristine water, moss-covered hills, and rugged mountains that jutted in and out of the coastal waters.

All too quickly, the summer drew to a close.

Unable to sleep my last night there, I pushed back the black window shades in my bedroom. There, the dusky light from the midnight sun shadowed the city. "How am I ever going to say good-bye to this gracious family who has touched my life with their hospitality and Christian warmth?" I whispered to Jesus in prayer.

The next morning after breakfast, we sat together around their living room table. Alf reached for his Bible. With tears welling up, yet maintaining his composure, he shared a verse from Philippians. Choking back tears, I read the words aloud. "And I am sure that He who began a good work in you will bring it to completion at the day of Jesus Christ" (Philippians 1:6 RSV).

I think what Alf was trying to convey through this verse was that though our paths might never cross again, we had no reason for saying good-bye. The Holy Spirit had brought our worlds together, and would continue God's work in us. The threads of faith and love we shared through the Holy Spirit would unite us always.

At the airport, I hugged them and waved a long, fond farewell. But I never said good-bye.

Prayer

Heavenly Father, throughout my life, I will meet many people and share life-shaping experiences with them. Although our paths may never cross again, reassure me that I need never say good-bye. Remind me that through Baptism, we are united in You. Help me share the joy of the Good News of salvation through faith in Jesus Christ with all my friends—the people I know and love for a lifetime and the people I know only briefly. In Jesus' abiding name I pray. Amen.

Journal Jottings

What enabled you to say farewell to someone you'd likely never see again?

Unquenchable Love

LETTING LOVE GO

Many waters cannot quench love.
Song of Songs 8:7

"How did you get over breaking up with a guy?" my college-aged niece asked me as we sat together on the patio. Although my situation had been different, I could still relate to the anguish she was experiencing over having to let go of someone she loved. So I shared with her my story.

My first day of student teaching, I wondered if I'd survive, let alone teach any grammar. While moving through the rows and answering students' questions, I noticed a well-mannered, good looking, quiet guy seated in the back row. After class, he waited for the others to file out, then walked past my desk. With a timid smile he said, "Goodbye, Miss Hill."

A few weeks later, he asked if he could come to my classroom for some extra help while he had study hall. After that he came like clockwork.

One day, he asked if I'd take offense being asked a personal question. I shook my head no. He wondered how I coped with my handicap. I told him how Christ daily supplied me with strength and hope to live with my disability. Then he told me about his brother's recent woodworking accident that had severed three of his fingers. After that visit, we never talked about faith or his brother's accident. The school year ended. I graduated from college.

Over the summer and throughout the next year, we corresponded on a regular basis and saw one another on occasion. During one of these times, he confessed his faith in Christ as Lord and Savior.

We became close friends, but by the following year, our relationship was developing into something more than friendship. Regrettably, I knew it was time to end the relationship, to let our love freely go. There were too many differences separating us. Trying to hold back the tears, I affectionately whispered, "We've become close friends because of our faith in Jesus Christ and the openness with which we've shared our problems. If God intends for us to be together again, somehow it will happen." Brokenhearted, we parted as friends.

I never expected to cross paths with him again. Every night though, as promised, we prayed for one another. Although we dated other people, our trust stayed strong. Song of Songs 8:7 says, "Many waters cannot quench love."

A year after breaking up, we wrote letters to each other that crossed in the mail. We sensed God had brought our lives back together. Gradually the affection we shared deepened into love. Five years later, we were married. Perhaps this wouldn't have happened if we hadn't given love permission to go away.

Finishing my story, I embraced my niece. Hugging her ever so gently, I advised, "Let your love go. If it's part of God's plan for you, He'll bring you back to one another with an even stronger love than before."

A sweet smile broke over her face and she jumped on her bike. I watched her hair whipping in the breeze as she pedaled down our driveway home. And I remembered well the journey.

Prayer

Thank You, Father, that many waters and many differences cannot quench the love You give. Ever remind me of the Source of love—the Savior who lived and died for my sins—and of the blessing of romantic love. Through Your love, I am able to love others. In Jesus' name I pray. Amen.

Journal Jottings

Reflect on an important relationship in your life. How is God at work in the relationship?

New Memory

*"As the heavens are higher than the
earth, so are My ways higher than your
ways and My thoughts than your
thoughts." Isaiah 55:9*

Whenever ten relatives travel for six weeks straight in two cramped VW campers, someone's feelings are bound to get hurt from words that are meant to tease. I recall such an experience.

One summer our family traveled to Europe. I was the lightweight, so I was assigned to bunk in the hammock of our camper. No one contested it. No one could. To sleep in this contraption, a person had to weigh less than a hundred pounds. The hammock was a temporary structure, not far from the camper's ceiling, constructed of a heavy duck canvas. It could be pulled out during the night to function as a bed and tucked away during the day.

Almost every night, long after the others had fallen asleep, I would turn on my flashlight and jot down the day's events in my travel journal, oftentimes recording how these incidents had enriched my faith.

One morning at breakfast, five weeks into our trip, someone started teasing me. "You'd think she couldn't remember anything. She's always journaling."

Another joined in. "Yeah, she thinks she's a writer."

I treasured my journaling time, so the remarks, probably intended to rib, stung deeply. It was a struggle to smile the rest of the day.

"Can any good come out of this hurtful experience?" I asked the Lord as I laid in the hammock that night, too upset to sleep. As I mulled over that question, I remembered the story of Joseph, a young man in the Bible who was much more than teased; he was persecuted.

Joseph was his father's favorite son. His father made him a colorful coat to wear as a sign of his affection. Joseph's brothers became jealous of the multi-colored coat. They plotted to kill him, but decided instead to sell Joseph into slavery.

Betrayed, abandoned, and separated from his family, this event must have wounded Joseph deeply, much more than a little teasing could. Yet Joseph endured this painful experience, and refused to dwell on the hurtful memory. Many years later, as a high official of Egypt, Joseph was reunited with his family and forgave his brothers. He provided them the provisions they needed to keep them from starving to death (Genesis 37–45).

If God could work good out of Joseph's monstrously painful event, I thought, *maybe my moment of teasing, although it'd hurt, could end up being happily resolved too.* I drifted off to sleep that night praying it could.

For the remainder of the trip and for years hence, I refused to dwell on this hurtful memory. I forgave my relatives, knowing that all my transgressions are forgiven by God because of Jesus' saving work.

A few years ago, I was entertaining at an extended family gathering. The conversation drifted to the trip in Europe we'd enjoyed together. To my surprise, the two relatives who had teased me the most about my nocturnal journaling enthusiastically inquired if I still had my journal from that trip. I did, and in a matter of minutes, I produced the yellowed notebook. For the next couple of hours, we took turns reading aloud the record of events I'd scrawled more than 25 years ago.

God's ways are higher than our ways. A new memory was made.

Prayer

Heavenly Father, Joseph's faith was so strong that even when he was betrayed, abandoned, and enslaved, he knew You would care for him. Give me faith like Joseph's, so when I am faced with hardships and hurts, my faith remains strong and I wait for the fulfillment of Your promise. As I live in my baptismal covenant and come to Your Table, remind me, Lord, that because You have forgiven me through the sufferings, death, and resurrection of Your Son, I can forgive others as well. In Jesus' name I pray. Amen.

Journal Jottings

Describe a time when you were teased to the point of being hurt. What good do you think has come of that experience?

White Porcelain Crèche

FINDING HOPE IN AN UNPREDICTABLE WORLD

Always be prepared to give an answer to
everyone who asks you to give the reason
for the hope that you have. 1 Peter 3:15

One year, while dusting my white porcelain crèche before Christmas, my cleaning lady asked where I'd acquired it. To sharpen my recollection, I pulled out the journal I'd kept while traveling with my family through Europe. Turning to the section marked "Germany," I remembered how the crèche came to be such a treasured item.

As I leafed through the yellowed journal pages, I recalled how our group had passed by a West German couple with their brood of children standing at the entrance to their cinder block home. At midday, they seemed to entertain themselves simply by watching tourists pass.

"May we come in and see your home?" my aunt asked the ruddy-complexioned, middle-aged man. Delighted to show us his simple dwelling, he led us inside. The bare walls, sparse furnishings, and well-worn rugs showed us that life wasn't easy for this family. Suggesting we sit down, he spoke in broken English about the unpredictable world they lived in.

Having a captive audience, he explained his point of view. "Several months ago, I was told if I paid one year's wage, I would immediately be issued a visa to visit my parents living nearby in East Germany—a country even more unpredictable than mine." He complied, but then was informed the rules had changed and he'd have to wait three more months. In the meantime, he had no idea if his visa would come through.

When the visa arrived three months later, the government official told him the rules had changed again. Instead of traveling a few miles on a direct route to visit his parents, he could travel only on government-controlled roads, adding some 500 miles to his trip.

On the day he left, he was advised he could stay with his parents only three days. Furthermore, he could not repeat this trip for three years, then only with a new visa. Even more painful than this, his wife and children would never be permitted to make the trip with him.

"How do you live in such an uncertain world?" my aunt questioned.

His eyes lit up, and he led us single file through a trap door and down several steps to a chilly, damp, hidden cellar. Camouflaged beneath a green wool blanket was a detailed, white porcelain crèche he'd sculpted. Gently picking up the baby Jesus, he mouthed the word, "hope." Tears welled up in his eyes.

With deep emotion, I closed my journal and said, "In a manger, hidden from this man's relentlessly changing, uncertain world, was his thread of hope."

This humble man looked to our Lord and Savior as the source of his strength in an unpredictable world. That night, as I gazed at the crèche this man had so lovingly crafted and given to me, I prayed I would never again let his message slip from my memory. The message of hope born in a manger.

Prayer

Heavenly Father, ever remind me that despite all the uncertainties of our world, I have hope and strength in

Your Son. And like the man we met in Germany all those years ago, give me courage to bring my faith out of hiding and share it with others. I offer You praise and thanksgiving for Your promises fulfilled. In Jesus' name I pray. Amen.

Journal Jottings

We live in a changing, unpredictable world. Where do you find hope?

Remember

Who shall separate us from the love of
Christ? Shall trouble or hardship or
persecution or famine or nakedness or
danger or sword? Romans 8:35

My family stood with other relatives at the entrance to Dachau, a concentration camp in West Germany, once occupied by POWs during World War II. Our guide was a chaplain and prisoner from barrack #26.

"It's a misconception that all prisoners were Jews," he said. "Many, like me, were pastors of another faith. Some were missionaries. Others were handicapped."

He explained that despite being poorly clothed, barely fed, and constantly threatened with execution, these people never lost hope. They believed they'd either be released to resume their free life or through death, they'd be released from this earthly kingdom and ushered into their eternal one. "Persecution as grim as this," our guide told us, "could not separate us from the love of God."

Closing his remarks, he said, "There is a great big ocean, between us, but I pray that you will always remember this place. Always remember the Holocaust and the atrocities it imposed, even when it'd be more pleasant to ignore it."

We were just what he'd said—a whole continent away, seemingly untouched by this tragic event in history. In my young mind, I didn't have a clue how this event in history could affect me. It was, as the guide had said, "more pleasant to ignore it." I scrawled the events of the day in my travel journal before I went to sleep that night. And like the sea that divided us, the memory was washed away until years later, when it resurfaced in another setting on a different shore.

Dad was having a suit altered by Mr. B., who was nearing the end of his years as a clothier. Mr. B. started telling of his days as a concentration camp prisoner in World War II. Dad, Mom, and I listened spellbound.

Down to a mere 70 pounds, his wife and son already executed, Mr. B. sat in his damp, mildew-covered, cramped cell awaiting the inevitable. Fortunately, for him, it never came. When his concentration camp was finally liberated, Mr. B. and 69 others were the only prisoners to walk out alive.

As Mr. B. paused, Dad asked him, "How did you survive such cruelty day after day?"

Without hesitation, Mr. B. replied, "I never lost my hope. I continued to believe I'd either be set free or pass quietly to the kingdom of God." With a resolute voice and an unflinching eye, he firmly cautioned, "Remember my story. Pass it on."

The words the Dachau guide conveyed to me so many years ago were brought back, clearer than ever. Hearing them a second time, I could no longer turn my back.

Perhaps it was because I'd grown older and realized more fully the historical significance of this event. Maybe it was because this time the message had come, not from a distant guide on another shore, but from a personal friend on my shore. Whatever the reason, for the first time in my life I realized such human degradation could happen again at anytime on any shore. And I knew that many who had endured this incredible hardship received strength through their unswerving faith in a Savior who had suffered even more to prepare a place for them in heaven.

For what other reason than this would both the Dachau guide and Mr. B., many years and a continent apart, have admonished me so strongly with the same message?

Prayer

Lord God, help me remember and learn from human history, even when it is more pleasant to ignore it. Never let me forget the hope grounded in faith demonstrated by people in such circumstances. And teach me to witness to the source of that hope, my Lord and Savior, Jesus Christ, who suffered so much for my sins that I may have everlasting life with You. I pray in Jesus' name. Amen.

Journal Jottings

Do you know someone who has been affected by cruelty at the hands of others? Tell their story, and describe what it says about the source of their hope.

Coincidental or Crafted?

RECOGNIZING GOD'S PLAN

As it turned out, she found herself
working in a field belonging to Boaz.
Ruth 2:3

Not long ago our Sunday school teacher asked, "Do you think things happen by chance or do you think God's hand is in them?" Some said "by chance," but others thought God had His hand in what we experienced. *What did I think?*

One day shortly afterward, while struggling with this question, I decided to read the book of Ruth.

Ruth, at a rather young age, lost her husband. She decided to stay and make her home in her husband's country with her aged mother-in-law, Naomi, a widow herself. With no one to support them, Ruth went to work in the barley fields, gleaning for leftovers. "As it happened, while she worked, she came to the part of the field belonging to Boaz" (Ruth 2:3 NRSV).

I noticed that Ruth "happened" to be in the same field as Boaz. Their relationship grew, and Boaz and Ruth eventually married and birthed a son. From this family line, Christ was born. I wondered. *Did this experience happen to Ruth by chance, or was it crafted by God as part of His plan of salvation for mankind?*

What about my experiences? Do they merely happen, or are they woven by a far greater plan than I could imagine? I found myself looking back in search of an answer.

During my student teaching, a young man in my English class inquired how I coped with my physical handicap. I shared with him how I handled adversity, which was through my faith. As he considered our talks, and through the working of the Holy Spirit, he came to faith in Jesus. Five years later, he became my husband.

A few years ago, I was in desperate need of a new leg brace because the one I'd worn for 15 years was beyond repair. I prayed and continually searched for a person to build a full-length brace. Finally I found Harvey, who had already spent a lifetime building braces. Bored with retirement, he had returned to part-time work.

Within a short time, he crafted me an almost perfect brace. A few weeks later, poor health forced Harvey back into retirement. He lived for only a few months more.

Ruth "happened" to be in the same field as Boaz. I "happened" to be in the same classroom as my future husband. Harvey "happened" to be back at work when I needed a new brace. *Did these experiences happen by chance or were they crafted by God who works in miraculous, mysterious ways?*

Through gazing back at my life, God revealed the thread of hope that ties my life together, and I knew my answer to the Sunday school teacher's question.

Prayer

Lord, thank You. As I reflect on Your Word and look back on the experiences of my life, I know that You are in control of an intricately designed plan created and woven by You into the tapestry of my life. Thanks for being my Master Weaver. In Jesus' name. Amen.

Journal Jottings

What is your response to the question: "Do things happen by chance or are they part of God's plan?"

One Opportunity

"Come and see," said Phillip.
John 1:46

While cleaning a closet, I came upon a box of catalogs and books I'd used as a learning disabilities teacher. Sorting through this outdated material, trying to decide if anything was worth keeping, I found a workbook of sample job applications I'd helped my students fill out.

I remembered Tim. He had worked so hard on these his last year of high school. One day, he loitered in the hall long after school was over, pumping up his courage to knock on my classroom door. Although I was tired and wanted to go home for the night, I let him in. Studying his eyes, I knew he needed to talk. I chatted about the latest school happenings, hoping it was enough to satisfy him. Before I knew it, however, he asked about my faith and shared personal spiritual questions with me.

Did I really want to share my faith with him, particularly in this setting and at this inopportune time?

Tim persisted. "It's like someone is trying to talk to me," he haltingly spoke. "It isn't cool to talk about a voice or a feeling, but I want to know what this is all about."

At that moment, I knew I had no choice. I remembered it was after Philip told Nathaniel about his experience of walking with Christ that Nathaniel then came to understand that Jesus was his Savior (John 1:43–51).

With the doors to other classrooms closing one by one, I stayed and shared my own experience of walking with my friend Jesus in as simple words as I knew. Just as Philip offered Nathaniel the invitation to "come and see" (John 1:46), so I extended this same invitation to Tim in those waning afternoon hours.

The school year ended. Tim graduated and enlisted in the navy. I never saw or heard from him again. Yet whenever something triggers a memory from my teaching days, like poking through a box of outdated school materials, I think of Tim and wonder. *What if I had given in to my desire to go home that day and never extended the invitation to him to 'come and see'? Would he ever have heard the Gospel message even this once?*

I am haunted most by the thought that I took only one opportunity to share this message of faith and hope with Tim. And I nearly lost that one chance because I didn't think the timing was the best.

I don't know if Tim came to believe in Jesus as His Savior. I hope and pray he did. But I do know that the Holy Spirit helped me speak the words of faith that Tim needed to hear at a time when he was open to hear them.

Prayer

Dear Jesus, open my eyes to opportunities to share what it's like to walk with You. Forgive me when I give in to my selfish nature and stay silent. Help me not to discard opportunities just because I think the timing is wrong, but to seize every chance to spread the Gospel message of salvation through faith in You. In Your holy name I pray. Amen.

Journal Jottings

When have you been given the opportunity to share Christ with someone? Share your happiness or your regret.

Six Hard-Boiled Eggs

SHOWING COMPASSION

Jesus said, "Feed My sheep." John 21:17

Whenever a beggar approaches me, I recall an experience I encountered many years ago in a country far away from home. The incident happened while my husband and I were in Japan visiting my sister and her husband who were there as missionary teachers.

On a steamy July afternoon in Tokyo, we were to meet John, a missionary friend, at the subway. The rush hour erupted in the already crowded, noisy subway, sending a deluge of people dressed in business suits scurrying to board the trains. As we waited, a tiny, gray-haired bag lady shoved her dirty hands up to our faces begging for a handout. Annoyed by the intrusion, we paid little attention to her.

After waiting nearly an hour, we wondered if something had gone wrong. Had we misunderstood the directions our friend had given us? Maybe we'd gotten the time mixed up. Perhaps we were there on the wrong day. Much to our relief, while wondering about everything that might have gone wrong, John finally arrived in his modest, compact car.

On our way to his home, he apologized for making us wait so long. We politely smiled. In his low-keyed, mild manner, he explained his tardiness. "While I was trying to find you in the busy subway station, a little, old, bag lady stopped me."

John continued telling us how this lady looked hungry, so he hurried to the market and bought her six hard-boiled eggs. When he returned, she was gone. He knew the delay would make him late in picking us up. He reasoned, "I was only doing what Christ asked me to do—feed His sheep. Sometimes it's as simple as giving a bag lady a few eggs."

So that explains why those six hard-boiled eggs were sitting on his car dashboard when we got in, I thought. In all likelihood, according to his description, this was the same bag lady who had approached us earlier. When we'd seen her distress, we'd looked away. When John witnessed this same anguish, he'd seen an opportunity to show compassion with a servant heart.

Through John's actions, Jesus seemed to be reminding me of His command to show compassion, to do "'for one of the least of these brothers of mine'" (Matthew 25:40). Jesus also said, "'Love your neighbor as yourself'" (Mark 12:31).

Loving my neighbor, I reflected, simply means showing compassion as an outgrowth of God's love for me every chance I'm given—even when my neighbor is an unkempt bag lady. It was a lesson I'd not soon forget.

Prayer

When faced with my neighbor's distress, Lord God, teach me to show compassion rather than looking away. Open my eyes to opportunities to feed Your sheep, to love my neighbor, as You have commanded me. Show me this act can be as simple as giving a needy lady a few hard-boiled eggs. Help me live as a redeemed child of God, ever mindful that in Your eyes, Lord, we are all beggars, continually in need of Your grace and forgiveness. In Jesus' name I pray. Amen.

Journal Jottings

When faced with a neighbor's distress, how did you show or not show compassion?

Raccoons from the Creek

EMPOWERING OUR YOUNG

*Remember your Creator in the days of
your youth, before the days of trouble
come. Ecclesiastes 12:1*

One misty autumn afternoon, I stood at the kitchen window, mesmerized at the speed with which the soft maples were dropping their leaves. My reverie was short-lived when a camper pulled into the driveway blaring its horn. Tumbling out the camper door, I heard my mom remind her 4-year-old granddaughter to close the door, "otherwise the raccoons from the creek, in search of food, will get in and wreck the camper."

Her granddaughter answered assertively, "No they won't, Grandma. Jesus is watching. Don't be so afraid."

Mom graciously went along with her granddaughter's view. Then, while her granddaughter was busy with her coloring book, she quietly slipped out of the house and shut the camper door. Before her granddaughter could even miss her, my mom was back. Climbing into her chair, this confident granddaughter gulped down her cookies and milk while Mom and I chatted over a cup of hot spiced tea.

Alone in my recliner that night, while waiting for my husband to come in from a long, exhausting day of corn picking, my thoughts drifted back to this young child's words. *When the "raccoons" sneak up on this child's camper of life, especially during those vulnerable teenage years, will she still remember to not be afraid? Will she still remember that Jesus is watching over her?*

Rolling these questions around, I began thinking of the numerous predators that might try to attack this girl's camper during her formative years.

Chances are, *peer pressure* will be an aggressive raccoon seeking entrance. Not even the crowd surrounding this predator can camouflage its boisterous voice, "Oh, come on. Don't be a dork. It's the cool thing to do."

Another raccoon that I suspect will try to gain entry will be *loneliness.* Its tone, unlike the first, will be far more quiet and subtle. "Why doesn't anybody like you? There must be something wrong with you. When are you ever going to start having friends like everyone else?"

Although I expect many other raccoons will crawl nearby, I imagine the one to be most threatening will be *inferiority.* It will give itself away by its deceitful voice. "Why is everyone else better than you? Aren't you trying hard enough? You're never going to amount to much."

I became apprehensive that somehow life would whittle away this young girl's innocence and the faith she now has that no matter what happens, Jesus is watching over and protecting her. That night, I went boldly to God, asking Him to chase the raccoons away from her life, many years before I thought they'd ever approach her.

That little girl has become a grown woman, safe despite the raccoons that tried to slip into her camper. Living as a baptized child of God and bolstered by a rock-solid faith nurtured through worship, Word, and Sacrament, she has depended on Jesus to watch over and protect her and to keep the door closed to predators.

Prayer

Dear God, keep me steadfast in Your grace and truth, always aware that predators like loneliness, insecurity, and pressures from society surround me each day. You are with me, protecting me from every evil with the shield of Your mercy and the promise of eternal life. Be with me, Lord, and keep me ever mindful of those You have entrusted to my care. Enable me to encourage them to be strong in their faith in You. In Jesus' protecting name I pray. Amen.

Journal Jottings

Write a prayer for a very young person, asking God to protect them and strengthen their faith in Jesus as their Savior.

Me–Have a Baby?

AN UNFULFILLED PREGNANCY

Trust in the LORD with all your heart and
lean not on your own understanding;
in all your ways acknowledge Him,
and He will make your paths straight.
Proverbs 3:5–6

"You can have a baby if you want."

After years of learning to deal with post polio-related problems, years of hearing we couldn't birth a child, finally we were told this joyous news. We left the doctor's office elated, anticipating all the wonders that lay ahead.

The next day, as I paged through catalogs of baby clothes and daydreamed of nurseries, the phone interrupted my thoughts. It was my doctor, the one who had examined me the day before.

Uncertain whether she'd clarified the risks involved with a pregnancy at my age and with my previous health problems, she'd decided to call me. She explained the likelihood of a complicated delivery and the potentially adverse effects a pregnancy could have on my health. Before she concluded the call, she reminded me the decision to attempt a pregnancy should be carefully considered.

I was stunned. My once bright future was darkened. All my suppressed dreams, so recently allowed to surface, had to be pushed away again. Or did they?

During the following months, I replayed the concerns raised by my doctor. Although my pastor kept reassuring me that God would reveal the answer, I found his assurance difficult to accept. As hard as it was, I tried to center my thoughts on God's will. *What did He want for my future?*

I read about Sarah in my Bible. I could just imagine how much she had wanted a baby. Yet when Abraham was told by three divine messengers that Sarah would give birth to a son, she laughed (Genesis 18:1–15). After all, she was nearly 100 years old. In her old age, however, she did birth a son, Isaac (Genesis 21:1–3). *This indeed was God's plan for her. Was His plan the same for me?* I still did not know God's answer.

Late one night while talking the matter over with my husband, I erupted. "If only I were 10 years younger, I know what I would do."

In a calm, steady voice, my husband slipped in, "Start trusting God instead of yourself."

I told him that's what I thought I had been doing. Together we read Proverbs 3:5–6, where Solomon calls upon us to trust in God instead of ourselves. For in God's grace are hidden the treasures of wisdom. He will make our paths straight.

After reflecting on that passage, my husband asked if I'd go with him to a convention. Some businesses were sponsoring a style show at the ladies' brunch where costumes from earlier productions at the Guthrie Theater would be featured. I told him I'd go.

Near the end of that style show, a middle-aged actress stepped out in a faded party dress that looked more appropriate for a young teen. The narrator explained, "This actress is dressed in a garment that once looked lovely on her. Now only its illusion of loveliness remains."

Suddenly, I saw myself mirrored in this person. Like her, I was still wearing a faded party dress—the dream of a pregnancy—whose time had passed. Its loveliness remained, yet it was merely a faded illusion.

When I least expected it, God had straightened my path and shown me a lesson in trust. Now, through His grace, I could move past my own dream and accept His will for my life.

Prayer

Dearest God, forgive my lack of trust and help me to place all areas of my life into Your hands. Increase my faith and give me strength to accept Your will and not dwell on my own. Take away my own selfish desire to lament what could have been, and lead me to rejoice in what is. In Jesus' name. Amen.

Journal Jottings

Do you have a dream for your life that is past its time? Make a note about it; then release it to God.

Broken Smor Jar
WHEN A CHILD BREAKS A CHERISHED POSSESSION

A gentle answer turns away wrath.
Proverbs 15:1

Our "chosen" toddler, typical of most children her age, liked to experiment with her new skills and grab any object in front of her. Realizing this, I moved everything out of her reach and left her in her high chair near the kitchen table to finish her cereal. Then I turned back to the sink so I could wash dishes.

Crash! Looking up from the sink, I glimpsed my panicky toddler trying to scoot away from the loud commotion. By the distinct sound, I already guessed what had happened.

While my daughter was dabbling in her cereal, she decided it'd be fun to nab the one object on the table I'd missed. When she did, down came the smor jar (butter dish) with a bang. The intricately painted porcelain jar my sister hand-carried from her choir tour in Norway lay on the floor in jagged pieces.

With a disgusted look, I lifted my daughter from her high chair. Just as I was going to scold her, I remembered an incident when I'd broken one of my mother's cherished possessions.

I was home on break from college. While zipping around the corner too fast with the sweeper, I caught my mother's favorite statue with the cord. The three-foot tall figure went flying to the floor. When it landed, several sizable pieces were broken off. I was angry and upset with myself. For several minutes I stewed, wondering how I'd ever break the news to Mom. I was already dreading her lecture.

When I finally mustered courage to tell her, Mom reacted quite differently than I'd expected. Rather than scolding me with the harsh words I deserved, she spoke gently. Quietly picking up the severed ceramic body parts, she put them in a box. She'd try gluing them together later.

I felt almost like the prodigal son who, upon his return home, received his father's loving reception when he believed he deserved something far different. I didn't deserve my mother's mercy, but because she loved me, she was merciful.

Until this moment, I'd never quite understood why she'd been so kind. Now I was beginning to. Mom knew how badly I felt about breaking a special piece of hers. She knew harsh words would hurt me all the more. Even deeper than this, though, I think Mom knew there'd be enough times of brokenness in my life—all the way from severed relationships to shattered ambitions. She didn't want an incident as trivial as this to be one of them.

Recalling the lasting impact of those gentle words, I swallowed my anger, held my toddler, and rather than punishing her, whispered, "Mommy knows it was an accident. I'll pick up the broken pieces while you play on your rocking horse."

While my toddler gleefully rocked back and forth, I picked up the salvageable pieces of my cherished smor jar and laid them in a box. Just like I remember my mother doing.

Prayer

Loving Father, ever guard me against leaving a "broken memory" with my child because of how I've reacted when she has broken something. Rather than scolding, teach me to speak gentle words of forgiveness. Remind me, Lord, that because of sin, life on this earth already brings brokenness. Teach me to show the same forgiveness and mercy You show me, although I don't deserve it, through Your Son's sacrifice on the cross for me. In the gentle name of Jesus I pray. Amen.

Journal Jottings

Have you ever left a broken memory with a child? What can God help you do to fix it?

Hand, Hand

TRYING TO SQUIRM FROM CHRIST'S GRIP

Do not now be stiff-necked ...
but yield yourselves to the LORD.
2 Chronicles 30:8 NRSV

The winter sun filling the sky all morning had by midday melted a thin, slippery film of water atop the snowpacked roads. This slick covering made driving difficult as I steered my car over the nail-biting two-mile stretch of glazed gravel to bake Christmas cookies with my mother.

Stopping near the sidewalk, I waited while my dad made sure his footing was secure on the treacherous ice and shuffled his way to the car. Unbuckling my 3-year-old daughter's car seat, he carefully lifted her bundled body to carry her inside.

Watching, I observed how my bouncy, bubbly, independent child squirmed in my father's firm grip, demanding to walk alone. In an understanding, fatherly manner, not wanting to stifle her independence, he set her down with great care. After scooting a few feet, her legs went out from under her. I could hear a whimper, "Hand, hand."

How much I'm like my daughter, I mused. Convinced I have the answers to solve my problems, I attempt to squirm from Christ's grip. I slip and slide along the road of life while stubbornly mapping out my agenda.

In prayer I tell Christ how, as Sunday school teachers, my husband and I are planning to take our high school youth on a tour of the church colleges near us. We have all the details worked out, so He doesn't need to get involved.

Again I pray, reminding Christ how my friend is scheduled for a biopsy in a few days. Since the doctor has assured her that nothing is suspect, He doesn't need to be concerned with either my friend or me.

Yet another time I turn to Christ in prayer, asking Him if He remembers the project I have due by the end of the week. Since I've already formulated my ideas, all I need to do is write them down. He doesn't need to become engaged in this situation either.

When the outcome doesn't happen as I'd expected, and my feet slide out from under me, like my young daughter I whimper, "Hand, hand."

When only four young people of a possible 12 turn in their permission slips to go on the college tour, I come running back to Christ, pleading for Him to take my hand. Sheepishly I ask Him, "How do we persuade more kids to come along?"

When my friend's biopsy comes back malignant, and a mastectomy is strongly recommended, worried, I return to Christ. Begging Him to grab my hand, I appeal to Him, "Help me get my friend through this ordeal."

When the ideas shaping my project flop, I come imploring Christ to reach out for my hand. "What kind of fresh, creative ideas can You bless my project with?" I ask Him.

I recall the time Jesus reached out His hand to Peter to keep him from sinking in the stormy sea. Peter had taken his eyes off His Lord and in that moment he began to sink. "Immediately Jesus reached out His hand and caught him" (Matthew 14:31).

Just as my father enfolded his loving arms around my daughter after she fell, so Christ wraps Himself around me as I bring my yielding spirit to Him.

I'm left to wonder only one thing. Why did I ever attempt to wiggle out of His hold in the first place?

Prayer

Forgive me, Lord Jesus, for the times in my life when my feet slide out from under me because I try to let go of Your hand. When the outcome doesn't turn out as I expected, and I come crawling back sniffling, You are there. You are present with open arms, ready to receive me unconditionally and wrap Your caring presence around me. Thank You, God, for opening Your arms on the cross and for reaching out to me with Your grace, mercy, and promise of salvation. In Jesus' name I pray. Amen.

Journal Jottings

Describe a time when you thought you didn't need Christ's hand, and believed you could solve a problem by yourself. How did the situation turn out?

My Daughter's Rescuer

LETTING GO

*For He will command His angels
concerning you to guard you
in all your ways. Psalm 91:11*

In my grandparents' house, hanging on the pale rose wall in the grandchildren's room, was a picture of an angel. This angel, with outstretched wings, hovered over a little boy and girl as they crossed a swinging bridge. When I stayed overnight there, I would lay under the covers, look at that picture in the moon's rays, and wonder if I had a guardian angel who watched over me.

After my grandmother passed away, I didn't stay in that room anymore, so I didn't ponder this question until my daughter's first day in kindergarten.

I watched through misty eyes as my 5-year-old daughter, dressed in purple leggings and matching top, confidently boarded the yellow school bus en route to her first day of kindergarten. We'd been inseparable until now, and I almost couldn't bear letting her go. Throughout the lingering day, I sent up prayers, thinking no one could take care of her quite like I could. I bugged God all day to keep her safe and help her adjust to the unfamiliar rigors of school life.

At 4:20 p.m. the phone rang. I knew my daughter should have been home by now. Quickly I picked it up and heard her shaking voice.

"Hi, Mommy." Pause. Someone, I could tell, was in the background telling her what to say. "Can you come get me at Cyndy's?"

Without hesitation, I assured her I'd be right there.

While driving home from Cyndy's, I asked why she hadn't come home on the school bus. She said she'd gotten on the wrong bus because she couldn't remember her bus number. When it stopped in town, everyone got off; she followed along. She walked up and down every block in town. Not knowing what to do or where to go, she finally sat down on a street curb to rest. Cyndy's teen-age daughter came to her rescue.

"That's when Heather found me, Mommy, and took me to her home. She gave me a chocolate ice cream cone and helped me call you. Do you think she's an angel, Mommy?" my daughter asked.

Before shutting off the lights that night, I whispered one last prayer of thankful blessing. "God bless Heather. You saw a lost little girl and sent someone to help her. Thank You, Lord."

Suddenly my grandmother's angel picture surfaced in my memory. "Are not all angels ministering spirits, sent to serve those who will inherit salvation?" (Hebrews 1:14). Today I'd received a vivid reminder that God sends His angels to be with us. Heavenly beings, who, when prompted by Christ's power, care for and protect His children.

For the first time, I thought I was beginning to let go of my daughter, knowing Christ would always care for her even when I wasn't with her.

Prayer

Thank You, God, for those who move among us, given and sent by You to protect and care for us and for our children. And thank You for sending Your heavenly angels. Because of Your gracious and merciful love for us, we as parents confidently release our children into Your utmost care and keeping. For You have promised to "give [Your] angels charge of [us] to guard [us] in all [our] ways" (Psalm 91:11 RSV). In Jesus' name I pray. Amen.

Journal Jottings

Tell of a time when an "angel" protected your child, or when you were a rescuer for someone else's child.

The Muffin Lady

JOBLESS

"To one he gave five talents ...
to another two talents, and to another
one talent, each according to his
ability." Matthew 25:15

I was feeling fragile and ugly, struggling with my inability to return to teaching because of my limited strength, when God sent a person into my life via television. Her name was The Muffin Lady. Her story was the catalyst that moved my life in a different direction.

Linda, a middle-aged southern woman, was the sole supporter of her family. When a massive highway project moved through her district, demolishing many area businesses, the company she worked for as a cleaning lady also fell victim. Out of work, realizing circumstances beyond her control were reshaping her life, she felt defenseless and vulnerable.

Resolved not to go on welfare, Linda began digging deep within herself for an answer. As she dug, the parable of the talents kept surfacing in her mind.

In this parable, Jesus tells of a man who gives talents (money) to three servants before he leaves on a journey. Although it isn't said, the man expects his servants to increase their talents while he is gone. The first two, who are given the most money, do increase them. Upon returning home, the master rewards them for their business acumen. The last servant, who is given the least amount, hides the talent he's given and does not increase it. The master deals this servant a severe punishment (Matthew 25:14–30).

As Linda considered why Jesus told this parable and what it meant for her life, she reasoned, "There must be a talent God has given me that, with His help, I can use in my present situation." After days of pondering this question, she arrived at an answer—baking.

In her past, she had enjoyed perusing old family recipes and creating new ones. But for years, the demands of her job and family prevented her from this hobby.

She pulled out her box of yellowed recipes and sorted through them. She came to her family's time-tested pancake recipe, passed down through many generations. "If I could use this recipe to make muffins, I could start my own business," she thought. Although a few of her friends thought she was daft for even trying, she defied them. Over the course of the next few weeks, through trial and error, she converted the old family pancake recipe into a new one for muffins.

By dawn every morning, using her one-of-a-kind recipe, she'd baked 400 muffins in assorted fruit flavors and her favorite, chocolate chip. By noon everyday, the Muffin Lady, as she became affectionately known, was all sold out.

Concluding her television appearance, she gave this advice. "No matter what hurdle life throws at you, and no matter how defeated you feel, I'd be willing to guess, buried deep within you, is a talent you barely recognize. If you excavate it, with God's help, your bleak situation can be turned around."

The Muffin Lady's story haunted me during the next few days. Finally I gave in and considered its message for my life. Although I'd suffered an indomitable defeat, one that had made me weak and insecure, by uncovering a barely noticeable talent, with God's help, my dismal situation could be turned around. God assures us that He is in control of our lives and has "plans to prosper you and not to harm you, plans to give you a hope and a future" (Jeremiah 29:11). Although we may face defeats and dismal situations, we can always be secure in our lives as children of God, adopted into His family through Holy Baptism.

Within weeks, after much soul-searching and girded with prayer, I began writing.

Prayer

Heavenly Father, sometimes unexpected circumstances reshape my life, causing me to feel defenseless and vulnerable. Still, I know that through You all things are possible. Guide me through Your creative power to unearth talents and strength, hidden deep and unrecognizable within me. Help me to discover my new identity as Your forgiven and redeemed child. In Jesus' name I pray. Amen.

Journal Jottings

Ask God to help you search deep within yourself for a talent that has gone unnoticed. How can you use it to further God's kingdom on earth?

Anything Extra?

TELLING THE TRUTH

Therefore each of you must put off
falsehood and speak truthfully
to his neighbor. Ephesians 4:25

Our elementary-aged daughter was delighted with the birthday gift we'd given her, a sparkling pink Barbie case. She'd dreamed of having one for a long time. As I tucked her into bed with her Barbie case clutched tightly in her arms, I wondered if she'd try to get it out of the house and to school with her the next morning.

The next morning, as my daughter was leaving to catch the school bus, I asked, "Do you have anything extra in your school bag?" She rebutted with a strong, "No," as she hurried out the door.

To be certain she'd told me the truth, I peeked into her purple school bag after school that day. Inside, under a stack of papers, was her shiny pink Barbie case. Without waiting a minute, I reminded her how the Bible tells us always to tell the truth. Then I asked her to go to her room to think about what I'd said.

Popping out of bed the next day, she tried the same trick again. This time, instead of the Barbie case, she packed the new pink T-shirt her aunt and uncle from Hawaii had given her. When I asked if she had anything extra in her school bag, she sheepishly grinned and bolted out the door with a quick, "Bye, Mom." I was certain she'd fibbed again.

Sure, I reasoned, she's only telling "fiblets," as our high school Sunday school students call them—little white lies.

But if I don't stop them, will she just continue to tell lies? How could I impress upon her the importance of telling the truth? As I was pondering the dilemma, I thought about another situation where deceit turned someone's life into constant struggle. It's found in the book of Genesis.

Jacob and Esau were Isaac's sons. The eldest, Esau, was the rightful heir to Isaac's blessing. But Jacob coveted his brother's birthright and deceived Isaac to take it away from him. To avoid Esau's wrath, Jacob was forced to flee from his home. Feeling frightened and guilty, he ran from one place to another a good share of his life until at last, thanks to Esau's forgiving spirit, the brothers were reconciled (Genesis 27, 33).

I thought about Jacob's lies and pondered how my daughter's "fiblets" may eventually turn into larger lies, perhaps creating a plight as disastrous as Jacob's. From the corner of my eye, I noticed my daughter dashing madly into the house.

With tear-stained cheeks, she placed the pink T-shirt into my hands. "I lied to you, Mommy," she confessed. "I'm so sorry. Please, please, please forgive ..."

Before she could finish her sentence, I threw my arms around her. Her conscience clean, she darted down the lane to catch the waiting school bus. A sense of relief washed over me as I started my new day, strengthened by the thread of hope in my daughter's future.

Prayer

O God, Jacob's story shows me the devastating effects of lying. Sometimes the only difference between whether children learn to lie or to tell the truth is whether we've taught them the value of honesty. Guide me in my efforts to teach my daughter of Your desire for truth. And remind me, Lord that just like Esau forgave Jacob, like You forgive me, through Jesus I ought to forgive others. In Jesus' name. Amen.

Journal Jottings

Describe a time when an older person reminded you of the importance of telling the truth.

That Woman's Big Mouth
DEALING WITH HUMILIATION

*"But make up your mind not to
worry beforehand how you will defend
yourselves. For I will give you words and
wisdom that none of your adversaries
will be able to resist or contradict."*
Luke 21:14–15

One mid-winter morning, while leading our women's Bible study group, I tried everything I could think of to hush that woman's big mouth. Nothing worked. Either she was reprimanding me for how I interpreted Scripture, or she was off on tangents far removed from the lesson. When I tried to bring the group back to the topic of study, she scolded me for interrupting her. Nothing I tried seemed to keep her quiet. By the time I'd finished the lesson, I was a nervous wreck.

Driving home, I became filled with anger, resentment, and heartache. I couldn't remember when someone had humiliated me more.

I was glad my husband wasn't home for lunch, as I sure didn't feel like eating. *Maybe if I get myself involved in something else, I'll cool down,* I reasoned, but to no avail. The disgrace I'd felt from the morning refused to leave.

Exasperated, I called a friend for advice. She listened intently and asked what alternatives I'd considered. I had two. I could go to this woman who'd wronged me and tell her tactfully how much she'd humiliated me. Or I could walk away from the situation, refusing to confront her, and risk letting it fester inside me.

"Well, what do you intend to do?" my friend questioned. I waffled, not sure of my response.

She reminded me what our pastor had said last Sunday in church. "But make up your mind not to worry beforehand how you will defend yourselves. For I will give you words and wisdom ... " (Luke 21:14–15).

After we'd prayed over the phone, I went to the woman's house, but reluctantly. I shuddered as I rang the doorbell.

Meeting me at the door, she told me, to my shock, that she'd been expecting me. Before we tackled the reason I'd come, she showed me an antique rocker, a family heirloom, and a scrapbook of family memorabilia she'd kept.

"You're not here to listen to me ramble," she spoke candidly. Before I could reply, she apologized for her behavior that morning and assured me she'd never humiliate me like that again. With that said, she shared some of her frustrations in growing older, anxieties that spilled over sometimes into our women's Bible study.

I stayed about an hour listening to this woman pour out her loneliness. As I picked up my coat to leave, she hugged me and thanked me for coming.

As I drove home, I recalled Matthew 18. "If your brother sins against you, go and show him his fault, just between the two of you. If he listens to you, you have won your brother over" (Matthew 18:15). Jesus goes on to say that "whatever you bind on earth will be bound in heaven" (Matthew 18:18). Unresolved anger and hurt feelings stay with us forever, but He urges us to forgive repeatedly, up to "77 times" (Matthew 18:22).

It was hard to go to this woman who'd caused me so much anguish, but it had been worth it just to find out she hadn't done it on purpose, as I'd accused her. It was worth, though, something even greater. I was reminded of Christ's faithfulness to the promise our pastor had told us about.

Prayer

Lord Jesus, when I think someone has deliberately caused me great heartache, it is so easy to give in to my selfish nature and avoid confrontation. But I know that if I walk away, I risk even more anguish and contempt. Dear Savior, give me courage to face people who hurt me. Help me remember that You will give me the wisdom and the words I need to clear the air and heal my troubled spirit. Show me how to forgive them. And remind me always that I am forgiven because You climbed Calvary to suffer and die for my sins. By the power of Your love, I pray. Amen.

Journal Jottings

Can you remember when another person wronged you? Describe your course of action and the result.

Shriveled Pumpkin Seeds

TRUSTING GOD TO CREATE

For we are God's workmanship, created
in Christ Jesus to do good works, which
God prepared in advance for us to do.
Ephesians 2:10

"Mom, can we save these pumpkin seeds? That way, we won't have to buy a pumpkin next fall," my elementary-age daughter asked after carving out the one we'd purchased.

"Honey, you know with my brace, I'm not able to plant the seeds. And that time of year, with your dad's corn planting, it's hard telling when he'll get to it," I apologetically responded.

"No, but Grandpa will help me plant these seeds," she countered with enthusiastic determination.

Never doubting, she carefully washed each seed, then gently placed them on a sheet of waxed paper to dry. After a few days, she moved the fragile, pale seeds to a pie tin where she watched them shrivel up.

With every phone call we made to Florida, where my parents were spending the winter, she reminded her grandpa about their spring project. When he and Grammy came home, Grandpa and my daughter would plant the pumpkin seeds she'd saved.

One fresh spring day, her grandpa made good on his promise. With a hoe and spade in his weather-beaten hands and the delicate, sallow seeds in hers, they made their way to the garden in my parents' backyard. He slowly bent down on his arthritic knees; she dropped to the earth on her agile ones. I watched from a distance as they planted the pumpkin seeds in the just-tilled soil. She beamed with delight.

My daughter didn't go to her grandpa's every day fussing over her pumpkin seeds as I'd expected. Occasionally, when she was there for some other reason, she checked them. Somehow she trusted God to miraculously turn these dormant seeds into pumpkins when they were ready.

On a blustery fall day, my daughter grabbed her grandpa's callused hand and led him down to the garden. There, no surprise to her, were five plump orange pumpkins. Getting the wheelbarrow, they hauled the fully grown pumpkins to the garage where her grandmother and I were waiting to admire them.

Like the pumpkin seeds planted in the garden, so God planted a seed of desire within me—a desire to do a specific task for Him. Although many people suggested I write a book, I didn't consider actually doing so until several strangers came up to me after a church workshop I'd given with the same request. God continued to plant seeds that matured me and prepared me for this task.

As He brought His plan to fruition, I understood the work He was empowering me to do, the "good work which He'd prepared in advance for me to do" (Ephesians 2:10, paraphrased). In God's time, He prepared me for writing this book, just like in His time the pumpkin seeds grew into ripe fruit. In God's time, he sent His Son to bring us to salvation. How long people waited for His plan to be fulfilled. Yet from the beginning God planted seeds for His plan of salvation, seeds that grew and ripened into the beautiful Gospel message for all mankind.

God's plan in God's time. This book. My daughter's pumpkins. Christ's birth, death, and resurrection.

Prayer

Like the seeds within the pumpkin, Lord God, You plant Your seeds within me for work in Your kingdom. Though the seeds lie seemingly dormant, You provide experiences that nurture and make me ready. When Your plan has reached its fullness, and I understand what I'm called and empowered to do, give me Your strength to do it. Help me to trust Your creative process at work within me. And send Your Holy Spirit to nurture seeds of faith in Your plan of salvation. In Your Son's name I pray. Amen.

Journal Jottings

Ask a child to plant seeds with you. Talk about how God plants seeds for doing His work. Write about the conversations you shared.

Winter Storm Advisory
TAKING A RISK

"Again, I tell you that if two of you on earth agree about anything you ask for, it will be done for you by my Father in Heaven." Matthew 18:19

It was mid-afternoon and a nasty, late-season winter squall was predicted to move into our area. We were under a "Winter Storm Advisory" and common sense dictated that I skip my last errand and head for home. When I looked at the light overcast sky, though, and didn't see any mist on my car, I didn't give it another thought. I headed to the greenhouse for a blooming plant to perk up my winter blahs.

By the time I left the greenhouse, a fine icy mist had begun to fall on my windshield. After carrying the blooming red tulip plant to my car, the greenhouse manager cautioned me, "This storm's supposed to get worse than they'd earlier predicted. With your physical limitations, I'd hate to see you get caught in it."

I thanked him for his concern, assuring him my car was prepared for a winter emergency. I knew the road crews would have the interstate cleared, and I'd be home in 30 minutes.

Inside, however, my stomach was beginning to churn. I knew I'd made a hasty decision to delay going home. Now I'd have to live with its consequences.

As I drove up the entrance ramp two miles from the greenhouse, I noticed the road was shiny. Ice was beginning to hang on my wipers. I turned on the radio to get a weather update. The announcer blared, "The Winter Storm Advisory issued earlier for our listening area has been upgraded to a Winter Storm Warning." He advised listeners to expect plummeting temperatures, dangerous wind chills, and heavy wind gusts. Due to heavy ice accumulations farther north, travel was not recommended unless absolutely necessary.

How could a storm come up this fast? I wondered as I shut off my radio so I could concentrate better on my driving and offer up some quick prayers. Mile by mile, as I traveled farther north, the icy conditions intensified, painting an ever thickening coat of ice on my windshield. I slowed my speed, letting the semi trucks whiz past me, leaving me temporarily blinded.

Suddenly, having been mesmerized by my wipers' monotonous motion, the obvious dawned on me. I could barely see where I was going. I realized my car's defroster wasn't melting the ice as rapidly as it was accumulating on my windshield. Either I'd have to pull over to the shoulder to scrape my windshield and risk getting rear-ended, or I'd have to keep looking through a diminishing amount of clear glass. Sensing I was only a few miles from home, I opted to keep going. I prayed, even more desperately than before, asking God to help me get home safely, despite the reckless decision I'd made.

When my preteen daughter heard the garage door open and saw me emerge from the car in one piece, she exclaimed, "I was so worried for you, Mom." She continued telling me how, all at once, while on the school bus that afternoon, she became very anxious for me.

"Did you start praying for me?" I asked. She told me she didn't know if it was a prayer or not. So I questioned who she'd talked to and what she'd talked about.

"Without closing my eyes," she responded, "I asked God to forgive my mom for being so stupid for going away in weather like this and to please bring her home safely."

"I consider that a prayer." I said, "Sounds like we were praying the same prayer at the same time for the same reason."

Sometimes, especially when we are in danger, we cry out to our Lord in fear and in need. The Bible tells us "Is any one of you in trouble? He should pray" (James 5:13). It need not be a formal or elaborate prayer; a simple request like my daughter's is sufficient. "The prayer of a righteous man is powerful and effective" (James 5:16b).

We hugged, both relieved the ordeal was over, both knowing why it was.

Prayer

Thank You, Lord God, for the people in my life who lift me up in prayer. I thank You especially when those prayers come from a child. Thank You for sheltering me from my own bad decisions and for keeping me safe. And I praise You for inviting me to come to You in prayer at any time and for any need. In Jesus' name I pray. Amen.

Journal Jottings

Tell about a time in your life when you needed prayers to help you through, then someone, perhaps a child, prayed for you.

Whole Picture

ADAPTING TO CHANGE

Delight yourself in the LORD and He will
give you the desires of your heart.
Psalm 37:4

"Roll down the car window," my sister motioned as we were pulling out of her driveway after visiting her family. "I forgot to ask you something. Do you care if we come to Florida the same time you're there to visit the folks?"

I began to feel anxious. Why couldn't they come a week later? There would be more bedroom space. Didn't she know I wanted to be alone with Mom? Such selfish thoughts raced through my head. How could I tell my sister the truth? I couldn't.

The night before we left for Florida, I talked with God. "Lord, why aren't my plans working out the way I want?"

I remembered the story of Jonah. Despite God's call to Jonah to preach in Nineveh, he planned to do his own thing and go to Tarshish. Jonah didn't want to face the situation in Nineveh. If he obeyed God and went to Nineveh, because of their pagan wickedness, he might lose his head. God interfered with Jonah's plan and sent him to Ninevah anyway (Jonah 1–3:3).

"I guess, Lord, I'm a little like Jonah. I don't want to face the situation I could encounter either. Although I'm reluctant," I relented, "I'll trust You to show me Your plan."

When we arrived in Florida, I noticed my sister wasn't her usual bouncy self. She told me she was going to have a baby, but her pregnancy wasn't going well. Throughout the next day, my sister's physical condition weakened. That night, while sitting oceanside at a restaurant where we were celebrating my 40th birthday, my sister suddenly turned pale. Grabbing my hand, she expressed how thankful she was for my presence. When she needed me the most, I was there.

Later that evening my sister miscarried. Coming back from the hospital the next day, she wept heavily on my shoulder. "My baby's gone, but you're still here with me."

Alone in my bedroom near the sea, I thought of what had happened. Once more, I talked with God. "Forgive me for my selfishness. If only I could have seen the whole picture as You could, this is the only place I'd have wanted to be—here with my sister during this difficult time. I'm glad You knew that and moved me in this direction."

Sometimes it takes an experience like this for me to realize that God hears my prayers, but my wishes don't always fit with His plans. Maybe this is what the Psalmist knew when he wrote, "Delight yourself in the LORD and He will give you the desires of your heart" (Psalm 37:4). His is the wider vision.

Prayer

Gracious Lord, sometimes I am so much like Jonah, thinking only of my own selfish desires. Forgive me, Lord, for my short-sightedness. Guide me to trust Your wider vision. When You change my plans in this life, help me to know that You can see the whole picture ahead of me. Enable me to willingly adapt my plans to follow Yours. In Jesus' name I pray. Amen.

Journal Jottings

When did you reluctantly do something you didn't want to do, yet strangely it turned out for the better?

Half Empty or Half Full?

My cup overflows. Psalm 23:5

Although I picked at the piano keys from fourth grade on, I didn't master the instrument even by the time I graduated from high school. I created many excuses. The two I used most were, "My sister's a natural at playing the piano. There's no way I can compete with her." And the well worn one, "I just don't have enough time to practice."

After high school, I didn't strike a single note until I was well into middle age. Unfortunately, my second attempt at learning to play the piano yielded the same disastrous results as the first go around.

"Why did I even try?" I asked my piano teacher after I'd humiliated myself in front of 100 guests at my parent's 50th wedding anniversary.

I recalled the moment. My daughter's fingers danced over every key perfectly when she played her piece. Then it was my turn. With my knees shaking so badly, I could hardly pedal let alone find a note. When it was over, I wanted to hide. No one knew what to say to me.

Looking my piano teacher in the eyes, I apologized. I told her I just couldn't get my fingers to do what my mind commanded. I couldn't play in front of people who knew me. "It's no use. I never could and I never will," I emphatically spat.

"Excuses, excuses," my piano teacher retorted. She said my problem in mastering the piano was that I was seeing my cup as half empty rather than viewing it as half full. "Focus your mind on what you can do instead of what you can't do." Her words reverberated in my head long after my lesson was over.

At home the next day while practicing, I thought, *Maybe that's why I never learned to play the piano while I was young. I focused on what I couldn't do rather than on what I could.*

I remembered my parent's celebration. *Maybe I didn't play the piece without mistakes, but at least I attempted to play it. Next time, it would go better.* Then God helped me see how I could apply this truth to so many areas of my life.

In my writing, did I appreciate the devotions I'd written that spoke to people's needs? Or did I focus on the paragraphs I'd labored over for hours only to discard?

And even more important, as I looked back at my life, did I see the person I'd become because I'd been handicapped? Or did I see the individual I never became because of my handicap?

I knew I had some mastering of the piano to do. Even more significantly, I had some mastering of attitude. With Christ's help, I'd see the experiences and circumstances of my life from a vantage point of my cup being half full rather than half empty. I would look with hope and joy at my life, knowing that Christ has made my future secure through His death and resurrection. For certainly my cup overflows!

Prayer

As I look at the cup in my life, Lord God, help me see what can be accomplished in the experiences and circumstances You lead me through. Fill me with joy and mold my attitude to perceive life as half full instead of half empty.

Send Your Holy Spirit to strengthen my faith and trust in You. In Jesus' name. Amen.

Journal Jottings

Jot down a goal you could realistically achieve within the next year. Practice a half-full rather than half-empty attitude. After a year, describe what you've discovered.

Three "D" Ghosts

The light shines in the darkness,
and the darkness has not overcome it.
John 1:5 RSV

One eerie Halloween night a few years ago, my husband, daughter, and I stepped hesitantly inside the haunted house our church youth had built. With sweaty palms and racing heartbeats, we read the sign scrawled in barn red: "Keep Coming Further if You Dare, But Prepare Yourself for a Horrible Scare."

Just then, one of the youth from our church, dressed in disguise, snapped, "Choose whether you want to crawl through the tunnel or walk the longer path, but don't loiter." Our daughter quickly elected to squirm through the tunnel. We decided the path, though longer, would probably be a safer route.

Venturing further into the dark commotion, the house picked up a wet musty odor. Our hands locked tighter. Suddenly, out of nowhere, a figure swooped down, pulling my husband with him. Another grabbed me from behind, leading me in the opposite direction into an inner chamber room.

Before long, I became aware of ghosts, clothed in their billowy white sheets, that lived in this room, a room dark, loud, and scary. Flashlights started popping on and off as these ghosts lit up their name signs. Three of the ghosts' names began with the letter D. These three began speaking to me.

The ghost known as Despair whispered as I walked by, "What's the use of continuing your life?" Doubt's ghost chased me around the room, continually asking me the question, "Are you sure you're a Christian?" And as I hurried past the ghost of Death, I heard him inquire, "How do you know there's a resurrection?"

Do I have any kind of defense against these taunting demons? I asked myself. That's when I saw the banner from our church hanging in the back of the room. Why hadn't I noticed it earlier? After all, it was the only area in the room bathed in light. I gazed at the words stitched on the banner as I mouthed them to myself. "The light shines in the darkness, and the darkness has not overcome it" (John 1:5 RSV).

In that moment, I knew that Jesus, through His victory over sin, death, and the devil, was the answer to any ghost, any demon, that sought to paralyze me with their fear. I'd been assured that the power given to me through Jesus subdues my demons and dispels my darkness. As Martin Luther wrote in his hymn, "A Mighty Fortress Is Our God," in referring to the demons in his life, "one little word subdues them." The ghosts must have sensed the power of Jesus' name, for soon they left me.

Christ, through the Light of His Word, had subdued them.

Prayer

No matter what demons pop up in my life, heavenly Father, seeking to paralyze me, be they the voice of despair, doubt, death, or whatever, clothe me with the garment of Your righteousness and lead me to call upon You. For "one little word"—the name of Jesus—subdues my demons and dispels my darkness. Through Jesus Christ, our Lord. Amen.

Journal Jottings

Write a question that the voice of despair, doubt, or death might ask. Now answer that question using a passage from Scripture. For example, "Are you sure you're a Christian?" could be answered with John 3:16.

Grace Defined
FOLLOWING THE STATUS QUO

From the fullness of His grace we have
all received one blessing after another.
John 1:16

I sat in church critically eyeing the 16-year-old seated in the front pew with the other confirmands. Today she'd be confirmed along with them. I was angry. This girl was being confirmed despite her unexcused absences from Sunday school, church, and confirmation classes. I wondered how the other confirmands, who had so faithfully attended, felt about this. Besides, what example did this set for my daughter who would soon begin her confirmation instruction?

Visiting with one of the deacons after the service, I questioned why this girl had been confirmed. "It isn't the way the church used to make these decisions," I complained.

The deacon explained the difficulty they, as representatives of the church, faced when making this decision. He clarified they could have chosen to hold this girl accountable for her attendance record and not confirmed her, or they could shower her with God's grace and confirm her.

How is grace defined? I pondered this as I thought back to a Bible story I'd often heard in Sunday school.

Zacchaeus, a Jewish tax collector, was in a crowd that had gathered to hear Jesus teaching. Jesus told Zacchaeus He was coming to his home. The crowd, despising tax collectors, responded with much complaining, "He has gone to be the guest of a 'sinner'"(Luke 19:7). But Jesus went to his home anyway. Zacchaeus responded to Jesus' unconditional love and repented of his sinful ways. He returned "four times as much" money as he'd unlawfully taken from the people (Luke 19:8 NRSV).

Zacchaeus had been touched by grace, I mused. The crowd only saw Zacchaeus as a sinner.

Hadn't I, like the crowd, only seen this confirmand as a sinner? Thankfully, she also had been touched by God's grace. He led me to new understanding of what it is to be the Church—a place where sinners come to be reclaimed through Word and Sacrament. A grace place.

Prayer

Merciful Lord, sometimes in my self-righteous desire to uphold the status quo, I become a barrier in Your church. Forgive me when I judge others. Lead me to be a woman of grace. Remind me that You have bestowed on me Your unlimited grace through the death and resurrection of Your Son, Jesus Christ, our Lord and Savior. In Jesus' name. Amen.

Journal Jottings

Tell about an incident when you showed grace to another person, grace that defied the status quo.

Odd

BEING DIFFERENT

I did not sit in the company of
merrymakers, nor did I rejoice; I sat
alone, because Thy hand was upon me.
Jeremiah 15:17 RSV

I had barely finished my dessert in the tea room when
my friend started offering ideas for changing the way others perceived me.

"Try being more humorous," she suggested. "When you
visit with a person, don't look directly at the person, rather
look away from them. That way, they'll feel more comfortable," she advised, as she continued on and on with her list
of suggestions.

Although she didn't want to hurt my feelings, it didn't
take me long to pick up on the underlying motive behind
her conversation. She was telling me I was different. To be
like everybody else, to blend in more, I'd have to make
some major changes in my life.

For the next few weeks, I gave her suggestions a try. I
tried blending in, hoping to be accepted more. For starters,
I tried to laugh at the mistakes others made. When someone told a joke, I chuckled at the punch line whether I
understood it or not. When conversing privately with
someone, I made sure I looked anywhere but at them. I
even put my devotional writing aside, thinking that was the
underlying reason people were perceiving me as different.
Yet I remained troubled.

One night, I shared my frustrations with my family.
Then, as if she'd thought about the problem as long as I

had, my teenage daughter said, "Just because others see you as different, Mom, is that any reason for you to change and become like them?" She went on to say there was nothing wrong with being different. "Maybe there's a reason you're different that your friend doesn't see."

After my daughter and husband had gone to bed that night, I pondered my daughter's words. As I paged through my Bible, I recognized many people from biblical times who God called even though they were different. Names such as Noah, Moses, John the Baptist, and Mary Magdalene leaped from its pages. One person, for some reason, stood out above the rest. His name was Jeremiah.

His contemporaries must have thought him strange, a person who would "sit alone" (Jeremiah 15:17), while all the people around him made merry. Perhaps he, like I, on the advice of others, had tried to change himself, maybe even dismissing his prophetic mission so as not to seem so different. God had used him, however, and had turned his being different into a strength. He alone was the one God had called to warn His chosen people of their impending exile because of their escalating disobedience.

In the quietness of that night, I realized my daughter was right. God could turn my being different into a strength, even though well-intentioned friends could not always see it. I didn't need to fit in with everyone else, to receive their acceptance. I already had unconditional acceptance from God. God calls us all, and through Baptism we are made His.

I breathed a sigh of relief. No longer would I try to be like everyone else. No longer would I put aside being a devotional writer because I perceived that it made me different. God created me His way on purpose, to do specific work for Christ. Why would I want to change anything as beautiful as that?

Prayer

Heavenly Father, remind me, there's nothing wrong with being different. Just because I'm viewed by others as out of the ordinary is no reason for me to desire to change. You have created me this way to fulfill a specific function in Your kingdom on earth. Help me to remember to always rejoice in Your creation and to glorify You in all I do. Lead me to Your Word and show me how to live abundantly in Your grace. In praise and thanksgiving, I pray in Jesus' name. Amen.

Journal Jottings

Do you ever feel different from everyone else? Explain why you feel that way and how it affects your service to God.

Our P.D.R.

HEALING LIFE'S DOLDRUMS

"Seek and you will find." Matthew 7:7

After one of those mega-shopping days before Christmas, my mother and I stopped by a coffee shop for a cup of hot chocolate before traveling home. A professionally dressed woman about my age, sitting alone, offered us two chairs by her table.

I used the standard opener, "What do you do for a living?" She told me she worked as a nurse in a doctor's complex nearby. That afternoon in the office's P.D.R., she explained, she'd been researching a disease which even the doctors she worked for weren't acquainted with.

Displaying my lack of knowledge, I inquired, "What's a P.D.R.?"

She explained that the letters stood for Physician's Desk Reference. She informed us that a doctor consults a P.D.R. when he or she wants a clearer understanding of how to treat a person's illness. It not only suggests medicines to prescribe, it also recommends other types of treatments to promote healing.

Surprising myself, I quipped, "Wish we had a P.D.R. for healing life's doldrums. I sure could use some therapy right now."

"We do," she assured me. "Why do you ask?"

During the next few moments, I opened up to this perfect stranger about how lonely, confused, and frustrated I was. I'd planned to resume my teaching career after my daughter started kindergarten. I hadn't been able to, though, because post polio had weakened my body too much. I left little unsaid.

This woman responded to my frustrations and concerns. "Our P.D.R. is the Bible." She went on to clarify how Jesus Himself is the greatest physician humankind has ever known.

"Yes, but He healed the body," I countered. "I need my emotions and spirit healed."

She continued saying how God could work this prescription to heal my spirit and help me overcome my midlife doldrums. Be it handling confusion, frustration, or finding a new purpose, a treatment could be found through Christ. She reminded me of Christ's words in the sermon on the mount. "'Ask and it will be given to you; seek and you find. ... For everyone who asks receives; he who seeks finds'" (Matthew 7:7–8).

With our cups empty, I asked the woman her name. "I'd guess you would say I am a messenger, God's messenger," she humbly said.

Over the next few months, I searched God's Word, believing that Christ had written a prescription with my specific need in mind. The Holy Spirit opened my eyes and my heart; passages that rarely spoke to me before took on new relevance.

If I needed assurance, 1 Corinthians 14:33 told me Christ wouldn't leave me in a state of constant confusion. "For God is not a God of disorder but of peace." When I longed to remove frustration, the words of Matthew 11:28 encouraged me. "'Come to me, all you who are weary and burdened, and I will give you rest.'" What about finding a new purpose in life? Jeremiah 29:11 offered most reassurance. "'For I know the plans I have for you,' declares the LORD, 'plans to prosper you and not to harm you, plans to give you hope and a future.'"

Increasingly, God built within me a confidence that Christ really did have a plan for my life beyond my teaching years. I discovered through reflection that "God did not give us a spirit of timidity" to pull back from life, as I once thought, "but a spirit of power, of love, and of self-discipline" (2 Timothy 1:7). Within me these very gifts are renewed and I remain in close contact with Him through Word and Sacrament.

Over the next few months of "seeking and finding," I felt a sense of renewal in the thread of hope in God's fulfilled promises. And something else happened. Something I hadn't expected. My blues began decreasing, just as the messenger in the coffee shop had predicted.

Prayer

Lord Jesus, keep me ever mindful that You are my source of power, both physically and spiritually. Keep me mindful that when You walked this earth as the Great Physician, healing the bodily needs of people, Your first and foremost ministry was to forgive their sins and heal their spirit. Thank You for the healing You offer through the spiritual P.D.R.—the Bible. Lead me to search the Scriptures with a receptive heart, finding in Your Holy Word a written prescription that meets every need my soul has. In Your Holy name I pray. Amen.

Journal Jottings

Tell about a time when the Lord provided an answer to a specific need for you through Scripture.

Love, Jill

Therefore encourage one another
and build each other up.
1 Thessalonians 5:11

After placing our food items on the automated grocery counter, I asked the cashier a genuine "How are you today?"

Unlike other cashiers who usually grunted a "fine" or "okay," this one wanted to talk. She told me how some customers had been surly. She just wanted to go home to her preschool-age son who was staying with a sitter. She noted that being a single mother wasn't easy.

My daughter, standing with me, became fidgety. She whined, asking if she could go to the car. I relented.

As I finished buckling my seat belt, my daughter said she was embarrassed when I talked to the cashiers while other customers waited in the line. Had I ever noticed all the people staring at us? Although I felt she'd exaggerated her point, she deserved an explanation.

"Did you ever consider that these people might be having a bad day?" I asked. "Offering them a friendly greeting, smile, or kind word is my way of encouraging them, building them up," I explained.

Still, as I unpacked the groceries, I thoughtfully considered my daughter's feelings. Maybe she was right. Perhaps I did embarrass her by talking too long to cashiers while others waited.

Not wanting to provoke or embarrass her any more, the next few months I scaled back my friendly conversations, preceding with business as usual whenever I reached a cashier counter. The only exceptions were the short visits I had with the grocery cashier I'd met earlier.

Several months passed. An early Christmas card with an unfamiliar return address appeared in my mail. I opened it and read: "When you come into the grocery store and visit with me, it brightens my day, although it sometimes embarrasses your daughter. Thanks! Love, Jill (the check-out girl)."

This note made me realize I should never have stopped trying to make people feel better, one person at a time. I thought of the people who were embarrassed by Christ's conversations with children, lepers, and other socially unacceptable people. He reached out to all people, regardless of their condition or station.

The Apostle Paul admonishes me in 1 Thessalonians 5:11 to "Encourage one another and build each other up." Does this mean I'm to do this even if it embarrasses those next to me? Even if that person is my teenage daughter? Yes, even then.

Prayer

Thanks, Lord God, for the many times in my life when You encourage me and build me up. Help me to never stop encouraging people and building them up. I never know whose lives I will touch and the impact Your love through my kindness might have upon them. Forgive me when I neglect an opportunity to show kindness. And remind me always to follow Christ's example and reach out in love to all people I meet. In Jesus' name I pray. Amen.

Journal Jottings

Ask a cashier, "How are you today?" Record the response you receive.

What If?

WORRYING AHEAD OF TIME

Then Jesus said to His disciples:
"Therefore I tell you, do not worry about
your life." Luke 12:22

A few years ago, my daughter and I were driving home from her dance lesson when she asked, "What if something happens to you and Dad and you can't teach my high school Sunday school class?" She knew we had taught this group for several years, and I guess she didn't want to be left out.

I was perplexed. *Why was she worrying about that so far ahead of time?* It seemed strange, until the reason for her question hit me. That's exactly how *I* had been acting. I'd been asking similar questions, worrying about future situations I had no control over. I thought about some of those situations, as she turned the volume up on her CD player.

In a few years, our daughter will be leaving for college. What will it be like for the two of us to adjust to living without her? How will we cope as "empty nesters"? Then there was the fear she'd often heard me express about living without my parents. What if something happens to my mother and dad? How will my life ever go on without them?

I asked her to turn down her CD player. We needed to talk about our "what if" questions.

I asked her what Christ's answer was to His disciples when they were consumed with worry about the "what ifs" of their lives (Luke 12:22–31). She looked at me puzzled. I continued, "Christ told them not to worry. He said they were to seek His kingdom first and all their earthly needs would be provided for them." I told her we are to first trust in

Christ's power in our lives. He will take care of all the "what ifs" because Scripture assures us that "Jesus Christ is the same yesterday and today and forever" (Hebrews 13:8).

I could see she was still uncertain. I tried to simplify it. "If we have Jesus in our lives, we don't need to worry about how our life will be taken care of. We have been baptized into Christ and know that He loves us enough to give up His life for us. Since He has provided us a secure future in heaven, we can be assured that He'll take care of everything we need on earth until then. We don't have to worry about the uncertainties of this life."

She asked, "Do you mean that I don't need to worry about what life brings until it brings it because Jesus will take care of it for me?"

I smiled my approval. And I resolved to model my faith and start showing that I trust Christ to take care of the "what ifs" of my life too.

Prayer

I'm certain that life on this earth brings changes, Lord Jesus. Since the future isn't mine yet, help me not to worry as if it were. Help me to trust that You will take care of everything I need as it comes along. Remind me that You have my best interests at heart. Strengthen me through Your Word and lead me to feast at Your Table. Send Your Holy Spirit to renew my trust in You. In Your unchangeable name. Amen.

Journal Jottings

Jot down some of tomorrow's "what ifs." Read Luke 12:22–31, then hand your concerns regarding the future over to your Father in prayer.

My Household Refrain

"I am the LORD, the God of all mankind.
Is anything too hard for me?"
Jeremiah 32:27

I was scheduled to fly to a Christian writer's conference, I was an emotional wreck. For some reason, I was afraid I would be killed in an airplane crash. I worried that my husband would be alone to raise our daughter.

Since I'd be traveling by myself, I worried also about my personal safety, health, and the weather. Every hurdle seemed insurmountable. For several days I'd been going around the house echoing the phrase, "I'm so scared." I'd repeated it so much, my daughter and husband had nicknamed it, "Mom's household refrain."

I'd talked with the Lord about these cares for weeks. I'd asked Him to let me know that everything I was asking myself to go through would be according to His plan for my life. Despite my prayers, I'd heard nothing.

While packing the night before my trip, I begged Him again to give me His assurance that everything was going to be all right—at least help me get rid of these nagging fears that the worst would happen.

After folding my last dress into the suitcase, my husband, daughter, and I gathered around the sofa for family devotions. Tonight, my husband had decided to read from our daughter's devotional book for teenagers. He began reading at Jeremiah 32:27. "'I am the LORD, the God of all mankind. Is anything too hard for Me?'"

Tears formed in my eyes as I slowly repeated His Words. "Is anything too hard for Me?" I rephrased it. *Is any hurdle insurmountable for Christ?* Of course not. Christ overcame everything—temptation, persecution, even the weight of the sins of the entire world. For Him, nothing was impossible.

God's peace came over all three of us as we exchanged gentle smiles. His Word had been given, especially to me. For the first time in weeks, I was calm.

The next week and a half went smoothly. There were no glitches in my flights. I didn't have to stay in an impersonal motel, as I had feared, but was housed with many others in a homey retreat center. And the outcome of the writer's conference was much more than I could have ever anticipated. To God be the glory!

Prayer

Lord God, forgive me when I let my fears get in the way. When faced with problems that seem insurmountable, teach me to look to You. Help me recognize that You come to me in many forms: Word, Water, Bread, and Wine. Keep me mindful that You speak that precious Word through family, friends, and many other ways, and that You use that Word to bring me to prayer as I experience Your promises in my life. Keep my heart, mind, and ears open to what You say. Lead me to always turn to You as the source of my strength, peace, and salvation. In Jesus' name I pray. Amen.

Journal Jottings

Are you feeling fearful about something over which you have no control? Write about it in your journal. Claim Jeremiah 32:27 as His word to you.

Scrawny Azalea Plant

WANTING MORE

Be content with what you have.
Hebrews 13:5

When I came home that night, exhausted from running errands, I noticed something new sitting on my blue gingham table cloth. Getting a closer look at its fragile pink buds, I gathered it was an azalea plant. *Where had it come from? Who would buy a plant so ugly? Why, it didn't even have a bow or colored foil wrapped around it to camouflage its scrawny appearance.* Curiously, I opened the small white envelope lying beside it.

Why hadn't I guessed? My husband always gives me an azalea for Valentine's Day, but he'd never given me one as sickly looking as this, I thought. Disappointed, I tucked the card back inside the envelope, determined to fake my appreciation.

Later that evening, when my husband came in after finishing his outside chores, he proudly presented the plant to me. I quietly acknowledged his thoughtful gesture. I must not have faked my gratitude enough, though, because he detected something was wrong. I whimpered, "For 19 years, you've given me the same kind of plant for Valentine's Day. You've never given me one without a ribbon or colored foil tucked around it though." He told me he didn't realize a bow and foil meant so much to me.

The next day, while still moping about the scraggly plant, my teenage daughter dragged in from basketball practice, lugging an athletic bag big enough to hold half her closet. Noticing my sullen mood, she asked what was wrong. I asked her how she would feel if her husband gave her the same gift year after year for Valentine's Day.

Quickly she responded by saying I was blowing this whole incident out of proportion. Rather than feeling sorry for myself, I should think of the women around me who would have been tickled pink just to have received a card on this special day.

"Mom," she curtly reminded me, "be glad for what you received. Don't crave more." With that slight reprimand, she left me to check her e-mail.

I collapsed in my worn recliner that night, intending to read the newspaper. Instead, my thoughts drifted back to my daughter's comment. Strangely enough, I remembered a parable Jesus taught.

A householder hired several workers to work in his vineyard. He agreed to pay them a certain amount of money for their day's work. All day long, he continued hiring workers, agreeing to pay them all the same amount of money. At the end of the day, all the workers showed up for their paychecks. Those who'd worked the longest, from the beginning of the day, expected to receive more than those who had worked a shorter amount of time. The householder, however, didn't see it this way. In effect, he said to the workers who complained, "Quit grumbling. Be glad for what you received. I choose to be generous with my payment" (Matthew 20:1–16, paraphrased).

This parable teaches about the generosity of God's grace, equally granted to us all. Along with my daughter's words, it made me realize that God was generous in His love. He had given me a husband who loved me enough to remember me on Valentine's Day. Many women hadn't even been remembered on this day.

I knew, too, that I shared a gift of love that I didn't deserve. Through God's incomprehensible love for me, He sacrificed His Son for my sins. I didn't need anything else. I resolved to start counting my blessings and be content with what I'd received.

As my husband watched me get up from my recliner to give my new azalea a drink, he heard me remark, "It sure is nice having a husband who remembers me every Valentine's Day with an azalea plant."

Prayer

Father, forgive me when I, like the workers in the vineyard, yearn for more. Remind me of the love You bestow upon me constantly. Most important, keep me continually aware of the gifts I receive through my Baptism, the forgiveness of sins and the promise of eternal life. Having been given these, I need nothing more. In Jesus' name I pray. Amen.

Journal Jottings

Make a list of all the blessings you've received this day. In prayer, ask God to help you not crave any more.

Miracles out of Tragedy

The eternal God is your refuge, and
underneath are the everlasting arms.
Deuteronomy 33:27

Around 11:30 that gray, gusty November morning, I received an alarming phone call. My mother's voice, usually calm, was shaking. "There's been a terrible accident on one of our turkey farms." Mom went on to explain what little she knew. A building had somehow blown apart on a farm where our people were working. She didn't know which farm was involved or how many people had been hurt. Dad had just called 911. "All we can do is pray and put it in God's hands," she said.

Weak-kneed, I put the phone down, uttering a frantic good-bye. With disjointed words, I asked God to be with whoever had been hurt.

I waited only minutes, but it seemed like hours before the phone rang again. To my overwhelming relief, it was my husband. He felt he needed to fill me in on more details. Three employees were nailing steel panels that had come loose on a roof at my nephew's farm when a section of the building seemed to explode. One of the three appeared to be critically injured. He'd call again when he knew more.

Awhile later, my husband called with more grim news. While this man was nailing the steel panels, a concentrated, tornado-like gust of wind grabbed the roof section he was working on. He was trapped in the steel and lumber debris. The violent wind carried him and the mass of debris

30 feet into the air and 120 feet downwind before he plunged, gravely injured, into the thick sod. The injured employee was en route to the hospital.

Two other employees, one of them his brother, had been working 15 feet away when the gust hit. A mere 15 feet away from disaster, yet they remained unscathed.

About an hour later, my husband phoned for the third time. Choked, he announced, "We lost him. The ER doctor said there was nothing anyone could have done that would have saved him."

As tragic as the situation was, two events happened that defied human explanation. First, approximately five minutes before the accident, for a reason he can't remember, my dad moved away from where he'd been standing by my nephew's pick-up. The debris that blew from the roof covered and destroyed the truck. Had he not moved, my dad would have been buried.

Second, at the time of the accident, my nephew and another employee were nailing loose steel on another building downwind from where the employee who lost his life was working. When they looked up and saw debris hurtling toward them, they covered their heads. The wind lifted the debris just as it passed over them.

Beneath it all—the untimely tragedy and the miraculous escape—were "the everlasting arms of God" (Deuteronomy 33:27).

Prayer

Thank You, Lord Jesus, for the security I receive from Your promise of salvation through faith in You. When tragedy strikes, I know that You hold me safely in Your everlasting arms. As I both weep and rejoice, I take comfort in the knowledge that You are my refuge. In Your eternal name I pray. Amen.

Journal Jottings

Describe a tragedy or an incident from your life that defied human explanation. How did your faith in Jesus as your Savior help you cope?

Mother's Brown Paper Sack

DESIRING RECOGNITION

*Whatever you do, work at it with all
your heart, as working for the Lord, not
for men. Colossians 3:23*

Stepping onto the back porch at Mother and Dad's home one Sunday for dinner, I noticed a plain brown paper sack on the settee. Nothing was said about it during dinner. After finishing the dishes, my curiosity won out. Slipping quietly back to the porch, I carefully opened the sack.

Inside I found a hand-tied quilt. I spread it out on the tile floor, admiring it. It didn't take me long before I noticed each scrap in every square was from leftover material my mother had saved when she'd sewn for my sister or me. Stepping back into my childhood, I recalled each piece.

The square in the upper right corner was a navy cotton remnant from a dress Mother had sewn for me to wear to my cousin's wedding. The day of the wedding, we left the dress hanging in the hallway at home. By the time we'd discovered what had happened, it was too late to go back and get it. I wore a borrowed dress.

In the lower left corner was a square of brown corduroy material. This I remembered as belonging to the miniskirt my sister wore for her graduation picture.

Even the retro '70s lime green upholstery piece was stitched in one of the squares. I just knew Mother would find a place for that material none of us wanted. I chuckled to myself.

At that moment, Mother appeared in the doorway. Looking at her tenderly, I asked, "What are you planning to do with this beautiful quilt that contains so many memories?"

Without any fuss, she told me she was going to drop it off at church the next day. I asked if she'd signed it anywhere since it'd taken her many hours to complete.

"Oh, no. I wouldn't do that," she said. "No one needs to know I made it. The only thing I need to know is that because I've sewn a few scraps of material together, some little child somewhere will be warmer. I don't need others to recognize my effort." Dad called from the basement for Mom. Our conversation ended.

As I folded the quilt back up, I mused how it wasn't important to Mother that she receive praise for her efforts from others. Clearly what was important to her was that she worked for others with all her heart, pleasing her Lord, as Christ wanted.

My mother's humble Christian service is a beautiful, inspiring witness to her faith. "This service that you perform is not only supplying the needs of God's people but is also overflowing in many expressions of thanks to God" (2 Corinthians 9:12). Paul wrote to the Corinthians that such generosity to others is a way of thanking God for His generosity to us. We are moved to share and care because God shared with us His most precious gift, His Son.

Carefully I placed the sack back on the settee, thinking about the thread of hope and generosity that held the memories in place. I prayed that God would work through me to model this kind of stewardship in my life.

Prayer

Thank You, Lord God, for ordinary, unsigned lessons that teach me humility in my service to You. Thank You for opportunities to share my blessings as a way of caring for someone else's physical needs. Create in me the desire to work from the heart, pleasing You. Keep me ever mindful of the gift of Your Son who cares for my eternal needs. In Jesus' name I pray. Amen.

Journal Jottings

Describe a time when you gave from your heart without needing to be applauded by others.

Carrying My Bag
NOT ENOUGH STRENGTH

"My burden is light." Matthew 11:30

Every time I left the writer's conference sessions to return to my motel room, I had to wait for the shuttle for at least 30 minutes, standing on hard cement with no benches in sight. When the van finally arrived, I'd have to climb four steep steps to get into the vehicle, making sure to throw my bag over my shoulders so I'd have my hands free to grab a seat. For others attending the conference, this was a minor inconvenience. For me it was a major ordeal. By the end of the second night of the conference, I was so exhausted I was almost sick. I didn't see any way I'd have the strength to make it through the remaining days.

Throwing my tired body on the bed that night, over-whelmed with the physical demands of the conference, I sobbed. I told Christ if I was to finish the week, I'd need someone else's strength.

The next morning, I visited with the conference director about my unusual problem. Although very much con-cerned, she had no solution. That day, I caught the van in the same manner as before, getting increasingly tired.

That night, after attending the evening's prayer service, Jane, another attendee, tapped me on the shoulder. Noticing how fatigued I looked, she asked if I'd like to ride in her van instead of waiting for the shuttle. She'd also invited Fran, another attendee, to ride along. Once Fran lift-ed me into Jane's van, I knew Christ had answered my prayer.

During the remaining days of the conference, the three of us made connections to ride together to and from the sessions. Soon we had the process down to a system. Fran, with her strong arms, threw my heavy bag over her shoulders, then lifted me up into Jane's van. Often, she'd even carry my bag to my next session. I soon noticed that when she handed my bag back to me, although it weighed the same, somehow it seemed lighter. My strength started to return.

After the conference concluded, as I waited under the shade of a magnolia tree for the airport van, I thanked God for sending me Jane and Fran, friends who had more strength than I, strength that carried me through. A thread of His hope provided through new friends.

Prayer

Heavenly Father, thank You for sending friends who help carry my bags—who lift my burdens when I can't. Remind me that I always have that kind of friend in Your Son, who is always with me, Who carried my burdens to the cross to reconcile me to You. In Jesus' name. Amen.

Journal Jottings

Tell about a time in your life when, through a friend, Christ lifted and carried you.

Crooked Christmas Tree

The angel said to her, "Do not be afraid,
Mary, you have found favor with God."
Luke 1:30

It was shortly before Christmas. I was recovering from a virus, my husband was pinch-hitting on household chores, and our daughter was tied up with activities. Knowing we were overwhelmed, my father offered to cut a Christmas tree for us. Little did we anticipate the tree he would bring home for us.

After propping the tree in one direction and then the other, trying to get the twisted trunk to stand straight, my dad had every reason to despair over the obnoxious kinks in the tree. But that was not his nature. Instead, he remarked, "Now isn't that the most beautiful tree you've ever seen!"

It was an example of the depth of Dad's optimism. He truly knew how to focus on the good he saw in every situation. He had the same response to the people he met.

I remember Gail, my dad's first employee. Gail had a lot of rough edges. But instead of pointing out Gail's faults, tearing him down, Dad articulated Gail's strengths, building him up. Because Dad continually highlighted his pluses, by the end of his stay with us, Gail's sense of self-worth had markedly increased.

The same is true of God and me, I thought. When God looks at me, He has every reason to see my defects. Yet that isn't His nature. Instead of looking at my flaws and foibles and tearing me down, He sees my virtues and potential, and builds me up. He even goes as far as speaking the same favorable words as He spoke to Mary, "you have found favor with God" (Luke 1:30). As a result, I too sense a greater feeling of self-worth.

Scripture tells us that God accepts everyone into His family. We are all sinners, we do not deserve His mercy—yet we are not condemned. Through Baptism and through Christ's blood, we are forgiven for our sins. God's unconditional love for us makes us strong. His grace eliminates our weaknesses, flaws, and foibles.

My dad had the right idea. Be it a crooked Christmas tree or a less-than-perfect person, God's forgiveness and favor let me point out the positive and forgive the flaws.

Prayer

Help me, gracious Father, to focus on the positives rather than the negatives. Help me communicate to others the same sense of worth You give to me through Christ's sacrifice for me. In Jesus' name, I pray. Amen.

Journal Jottings

The next time you're tempted to focus on life's minuses, think about God's grace in your life. Write your reflections.

Not Right Now

MESSING UP MY ROUTINE

He said to them, "Let the little children
come to me, and do not hinder them."
Mark 10:14

Munching hamburgers before the opening game of the spring softball season, I cheerfully asked the woman behind me if she was looking forward to the school year being over.

She curtly replied, "No. The girls will be home. It will just mess up my routine." Jolted, I thought back to a time several years ago when I felt the same way.

"Mommy, my new friend has come to play with me," my daughter announced excitedly.

In a disinterested tone I asked her, "What's your name?" Barely waiting for a response, I suggested they go outside and swing while I continued my work. Sensing I had no time for them, they picked up their purple backpacks and went outside. I went back to my work.

A few minutes later, I heard the door slam, then I felt a tap on my shoulder. Looking up, I saw my daughter's restless eyes telling me she was bored. She begged me to come outside and color with them in their brand new coloring books. I brushed her off, "Not right now, Honey." She quietly left.

This time when I returned to my work, I saw in my mind the picture that hangs in our church of Jesus blessing the little children—not turning them away. *Jesus welcomed them,* I reflected, *unlike the disciples, who tried to send the children away.* In those days, children would have been considered a disruption, but Jesus recognized the importance of stopping His routine for them. He wanted to bless them and teach them, because even young children can understand the depth of His love. And by doing so, Jesus taught His disciples—and us—that the message of salvation through faith in Him is for everyone.

I hung my head in shame that I'd been so self-centered and worried about my daughter and her friend interrupting my routine.

Just then the rap of a tiny fist against the windowpane captured my attention. I read my daughter's lips. "Do you have any cookies, Mommy?"

I threw open the window and replied, "Sure do. Let's have a tea party." I told her to get their dolls ready, and I'd be right out with some punch and cookies.

I'll never forget the grin on my daughter's face.

Prayer

Teach me, Lord God, to learn how to bless my child despite my overbooked schedules and pressing routines. By seeing things through her playful eyes, may my world and my problems seem a little lighter and easier to handle. Remind me that no one is insignificant in Your eyes, that salvation through faith in Jesus is for everyone, young and old. In Jesus' name I pray. Amen.

Journal Jottings

Take time from your busy schedule to play with a child. Note something you both gained from this experience.

"It's His Mistake"

TAKING THE RAP

*"Why do you look at the speck of
sawdust in your brother's eye and
pay no attention to the plank in your
own eye?" Matthew 7:3*

My husband offered to go to the bank and make the deposit before he went to his meeting, so I wouldn't need to go in later during the day. I gratefully accepted.

When he left, I assumed he'd be gone all day. Soon he returned and handed me the deposit book. I was puzzled. He said the people riding with him weren't ready when he stopped by, so he decided to rush home with the deposit book. "This way, you'll be able to balance the checkbook before I get home tonight, Honey," he explained with a quick kiss good-bye.

Later that day, while doing my bookkeeping chores, I discovered the numbers my husband had recorded in the deposit book didn't match the numbers on the check stub. "And I've already recorded that deposit in the checkbook and balanced the transactions that followed it," I fussed.

Sure enough, when I called the bank, I found out my husband had made a mistake. Evidently when he hurriedly wrote the figure in the deposit book, he'd transposed three of the numbers. After my call, the bank went to work correcting the mistake in their computer.

Opening the checkbook, I sputtered, "If he hadn't made such a stupid error, I wouldn't have to redo all these figures. Besides, when I get done, the checkbook will look like an amateur was in charge of it."

I was right. After I finished, my checkbook looked anything but what I'd call neat. I had a choice. Either I could make this look like my mistake and leave no note of explanation. Or I could add a note in the checkbook explaining whose mistake this really was. If I chose the latter, I knew my husband would take the rap when my dad recorded checks in the general ledger at the end of the month.

Determined to set the record straight, I grabbed a self-stick note to write on. Before I could stick it in the checkbook, however, I remembered the question Jesus once asked His followers. "Why do you see the speck in your neighbor's eye, but do not notice the log in your own eye?" (Matthew 7:3 NRSV).

Why did I see this one error my husband had made, yet I failed to see all the mistakes I'd made which he had overlooked? I was humbled even more when I thought how God made it possible for us to enter His kingdom—through the way of the cross. If I looked at the record of my life, I would not see mistakes or notes explaining whose fault it was. I would see a clean slate, made so by the blood of our Savior.

After that, there was no need to put a note in the checkbook.

Prayer

Dearest Savior, there are times when I want to set the record straight, to point out that I'm not at fault. Make me aware, Lord, of the plank that is in my own eye. Remind me that You have already wiped out my mistakes. And remind me how You took the ultimate rap for me, by dying on the cross as payment for my sins. In Your name I pray. Amen.

Journal Jottings

Tell about a time when you took the rap for someone else and what made you decide to do this.

Life's Passing Squalls

SCRAMBLING TO HOLD LIFE TOGETHER

He got up, rebuked the wind and said to
the waves, "Quiet! Be still!" Mark 4:39

"I was scrambling just to hold my life together." How
many times I've echoed these thoughts as I've confronted
life's storms. One such squall occurred when we struggled
with changes in our business.

Raising turkeys was our mainstay. When the company
that had been contracting and marketing our birds closed,
we, along with other area growers, had no choice than to
buy the processing plant. We had to have a place to market our turkeys. After operating the plant just a few weeks,
the turkey market plummeted to an all-time low. Before we
knew it, we were scrambling just to hold our lives together, to keep our livelihood and our family farm intact. The
wind and the waves were pounding our boat from all
directions, or so it seemed.

Amid this turbulence, I remembered another boat at
another time getting pounded. Jesus' disciples must have
been scrambling to save their lives that night when a
vicious storm arose at sea. Scripture tells us that the disciples woke Jesus and asked if He didn't care if they
drowned.

Jesus moved into their storm, their predicament. He got
up, Scripture records, "rebuked the wind and said to the
waves, 'Quiet! Be still!' Then the wind died down and it
was completely calm" (Mark 4:39). Jesus quieted the storm
and restored life back to usual.

As He did with the disciples, so the Lord did with the storm affecting our life. Gradually, He stepped into our storm and manifested His presence. Calmly, slowly, He hushed the winds and waves buffeting our family's boat. As time passed, He made circumstances happen so we were able to keep our farm intact. He brought peace and stability back to our lives, allowing us to sail on calmer waters.

I'm very much aware, however, that Christ doesn't always calm our storms the way we think He should. He always moves into them, manifesting His presence and power according to *His* directive, not ours. And although we know that there will be storms in this life, we can be secure in the knowledge that we are safe from the ultimate storm—separation from God. Jesus protects us from sin's high winds and waves because He gave Himself for us. And He calms us with three simple words, "Peace! Be still!" (Mark 4:39 RSV).

Prayer

When I am storm-tossed upon the sea of life, Lord Jesus, scrambling just to hold my life together, thank You for Your presence. You calm each storm that confronts me according to Your directive. You restore peace and stability, permitting me to sail on calmer waters. Remind me that You alone are the source of strength and salvation. For the way that You work in my life, I give You my humble praise. In Your holy name I pray. Amen.

Journal Jottings

When has Christ moved into your life calming what once was turbulent?

Lost Woman

WITNESSING THROUGH SILENCE

"You did not choose me, but I chose you
and appointed you to go and bear
fruit—and that fruit will last."
John 15:16

I dialed my mom telling her how our daughter was writing her "affirmation of faith" speech on the question, "Can we witness for Christ through our silence?" I wondered if Mom could offer her any suggestions.

"Before she writes anymore, let me tell you about an incident that happened to me awhile back," Mom said.

A few months earlier, when she was wintering with Dad in Florida, Mom decided to take a walk on the beach. While strolling by herself along the shoreline, watching the sandpipers skitter back and forth, she came upon an elderly woman who looked scared and disoriented. As she drew closer, she heard the older woman mumbling, "I think I lost my family."

Mom asked the woman, "Where were you when you became separated from your family?"

The woman wasn't sure. Mom pulled her sweatshirt off and placed it on the woman's bare, shivering shoulders. "Here, you need it more than I do," she insisted. Slowly, the woman started to relax.

After walking almost a mile on the beach, searching for this lost woman's family, my mother spotted a rest area nearby where there was a phone. While she called 911, the woman sprawled out on a park bench.

"This woman's family has been in touch with the police trying to establish her whereabouts," the 911 dispatcher explained. The dispatcher asked Mother to stay with this woman until the police and her two sons arrived. Within minutes, the woman was united with her family. Mom tenderly put her arms around the woman. The woman gave my mother a tight squeeze in response. Her actions, not her words, had spoken her witness to love through Christ.

After Mom finished her story, she asked me to share it with my daughter when she returned home from school. "Maybe it will help her decide whether we can witness for Christ through our silence," Mom offered.

I realized then, that through the simple act of helping my daughter with her own work, I had been blessed too. My mother's story helped me reaffirm my own faith. And I knew the answer to my daughter's question.

Prayer

Gracious God, I know that I can witness my faith in so many ways. Show me how to share Your message of hope and salvation with others, even when it doesn't seem to be an obvious time. Use my words and actions to tell others about Your faithfulness. In Jesus' name I pray. Amen.

Journal Jottings

Write your answer to the question, "Can we witness for Christ through our silence?"

Sack of Work Clothes

RESPONDING TO ANOTHER'S NEEDS

*"Whatever you did for one of the least of
these brothers of mine, you did for me."*
Matthew 25:40

An employee of our farming organization knocked on
the screen door of our ranch home. He was there to collect
his last paycheck.

When I opened the door, I noticed he was holding in
his arms a plain brown paper grocery sack. The bulging
sack held the five sets of nearly new work clothes we had
provided to him as an employee. With downcast eyes, he
hesitated before he spoke. "These are the nicest clothes
I've ever had. I wish I didn't have to give them back." It
was our policy that when people left our employment, they
returned the clothes we provided.

Feeling sorry for him standing there in the late March
drizzle, I asked if he wanted to step inside while I wrote
his paycheck. He followed me in and took the chair I
offered, still hugging the sack as if it were his best friend.
I noticed that he quietly studied the comforts of my home.
Although my heart still hurt for him, I remained silent and
did nothing.

After I finished writing his check, he got up and tucked
it carefully into his patched shirt pocket. *That shirt may be
the only one he owns,* I thought. Opening the door to leave,
he clutched his sack even tighter as if to say his final good-
bye. Before reaching the screen door that led outside, he
slowly and obediently set the sack down. With one final
glance back at me, he left.

I slowly closed the kitchen door. In the distance I could almost see the face of Jesus and hear Him reminding me, "Whatever you did for one of the least of these brothers of mine, you did for me" (Matthew 25:40). Recalling these words, I felt full of regret, knowing it was too late to let the man keep the work clothes. I chastised myself—*couldn't I have let him keep these used work clothes if they meant so much to him, despite our company's usual policy?*

Sitting at my desk to write the other paychecks, I asked the Lord to help me keep a new promise—that the next time someone came to me in need, I would give what I could. I didn't want to miss another opportunity to serve Jesus by serving others.

Prayer

Forgive me, Lord Jesus, for the many times in my life that a person in need has come to me, and I have done nothing. Remind me that before Your eyes I am needy too, in need of Your continual grace and forgiveness. Thank You for never turning me away, and for redeeming me through the gift of Your precious blood. In Your holy name I pray. Amen.

Journal Jottings

Write about a time when a needy person came to you, and how you responded.

Battered Wooden Chest

*"The people living in darkness have seen
a great light." Matthew 4:16*

A group of family and friends gathered in my aunt and uncle's cozy home to see my cousin's slides. Home on furlough as a missionary teacher in a country where Christianity is not openly practiced, she captivated us with her moving stories. Spellbound, we listened to her tell about the night she had an unexpected visitor.

It was around 9:30 p.m. when she heard a faint knock on her apartment door. In the darkened hall stood a middle-aged woman she recognized as an administrator at the university where she taught. Knowing her apartment was electronically bugged, she thought it might be a set-up to find a reason to deport her from the country. So it was with reluctance that she let this woman in.

Immediately this woman began pouring out her life's story. She told how her parents had forced her to marry someone she didn't love and how she'd been unfaithful to him. Now her life seemed empty and meaningless. She knew there had to be more to life than this darkness.

Still cautious, my cousin opened her Bible and explained passages that offered hope in Jesus Christ. Although it was risky to possess a Bible, she gave the woman her only Bible, telling her to go home and continue searching for the answers to her many questions.

Two nights later, after devouring the contents of the loaned Bible, this woman returned and asked my cousin if she could find her a Bible to keep. Realizing how difficult it was to secure a Bible in this country, she hesitatingly agreed.

Several weeks passed. One late afternoon, after bicycling many rut-filled miles to find medicine for a friend, my cousin met a doctor. As they conversed, she discovered he too was a Christian. After explaining how she needed to find a Bible for this university administrator, he took her to his home. There, he opened a battered wooden chest. Stacked inside were a number of Bibles in various translations and versions.

"Where did they all come from?" she asked.

He explained he had a non-Christian friend working at the border. Every time he confiscated a Bible he didn't know what to do with, he gave it to the doctor just to get rid of it. The doctor in turn passed the Bibles to Christian friends who secretly distributed them within the country. God had His way of keeping His Word alive even in this country gripped by darkness.

Despite the risk involved, my cousin hand-delivered one of these Bibles the next day to the university administrator. Before she left on furlough, she also made sure this woman had another person available with whom she could discuss the Scripture verses.

Long after the slides were put away, I recalled her story. This woman bravely knocked on my cousin's door one night in search of answers. God instilled within her a courageous, willing spirit, and she received her own Bible—a source of light in her once darkened world, a thread of hope that ties her to God's promise of salvation. I prayed that the Holy Spirit would instill that kind of courage in me.

Prayer

Lord God, in this country I am free to share Your Holy Word with anyone. Despite this, there are times that political, emotional, and even religious barriers prevent me from sharing the Gospel message. Give me the courage, Lord, to risk whatever it takes to spread the Good News to our darkened world. Help me help those who serve You in other lands to share the Light of the world. Assure me You stand by me and will provide ways to keep Your Word alive. In Jesus' name I pray. Amen.

Journal Jottings

Tell about the risks you take to spread God's Word to the darkened world.

Elusive Dreams

DREAMS THAT DON'T COME TRUE

"Call upon Me in the day of trouble;
I will deliver you, and you shall
honor Me." Psalm 50:15

My friend had interviewed for a new managerial position. Her resume of past experiences, before her two children were born, fit the job description perfectly. It came as no surprise when she called to tell me she'd been offered the job.

The news left me feeling elated for my friend but hurt and empty inside. Hurt because we'd no longer have as much time for our friendship. Empty because, well that went much deeper. The prospect of my friend taking a new job triggered a grief within me I thought I'd banished years ago.

By the time I'd raised my daughter to elementary age, when I was the same age my friend was now, I too had dreamed of finding a new job. I'd envisioned myself returning to teaching, the career I'd left behind for motherhood. When that time came, however, post polio had taken its toll on me and that dream was never realized.

With the telephone receiver still warm from our conversation, I lamented, *Why do dreams like this become a reality for almost everyone else, but elude me?* While I rejoiced with my friend, I grieved anew for my unfulfilled dream.

At the same time my friend was adjusting to her new job and I was recovering from my heartache, two of my nieces announced they were pregnant. Both were expecting near my birthday. Another silent pain set in. This time an emptiness even more profound penetrated deeper.

When I'd been the same age as my nieces, I had dreamed of conceiving a child. I'd always been curious how I'd look and feel being pregnant. *Who would our child resemble? What personality traits would our child inherit?* Far more important, though, I desired the deeply personal experience of having God create a life within me.

On the advice of many doctors, though, I'd been persuaded to let go of this dream too. Still, after all these years—even after God had blessed us with a precious, adopted daughter who is our delight and all God intended—I yearned, at moments like these, for my derailed dream. While I shared joy for the upcoming births of my nieces' first babies, I grieved for the dream that had evaded me.

So many of my dreams had passed me by. From this abyss, I cried to God for deliverance, asking that the dream closest to my heart right then would not elude me too. As I did, I recalled the dream God had fulfilled in Hannah, Sarah, and Elizabeth, biblical women well into their journey of life. *Would God fulfill my deepest desire as well?* I wondered.

A few days later, my daughter, sprinting in with the mail, exclaimed with the widest grin, "Mom, you received a large envelope from a publisher."

My heart skipped a beat. "Are the contents a book contract or a returned book proposal?" I questioned as I limped wildly to the kitchen. Hastily, I opened the oversized envelope—out dropped a contract. My daughter and I shouted with joy.

A dream, close to my heart, had finally been realized and fulfilled in God's time. He made it possible for me to pick up the thread of hope again.

Prayer

Soothe my troubled heart, dearest God, when it seems that the fulfillment of my dreams elude me yet happen to everyone else. Remind me that You work in all things for my good. In Your kindness, make Your will known to me and equip me to do Your work. Send Your Holy Spirit to strengthen my faith and trust, keeping me ever close to You. In Jesus' name I pray. Amen.

Journal Jottings

Write about the dream closest to your heart right now. Write a prayer placing your dream in God's hands.

An Accepting Heart
PRACTICING TOLERANCE

*"So in everything, do to others what
you would have them do to you."*
Matthew 7:12

I was elated for my friend. The last time she visited, she announced that after having spent several summers studying and teaching, this summer she was planning to take it easier and spend it with her children. Both kids were preschoolers.

One day, however, I received an e-mail stating her plans had changed. A university professor, she'd been offered an opportunity to write a textbook for a well-respected company. In two weeks, she'd be flying to the East Coast to sign a contract.

I fumed that she'd made the wrong decision as I tucked my preteen daughter into bed. Before I turned out the lights, I asked what she thought of my friend's plans. Assuming she'd echo my point of view, I was surprised at her reaction.

"Maybe it's right in your friend's heart for her to write a textbook this summer," my daughter said. "Maybe it's just not right in yours, Mom. If you still want her friendship, you need to just accept it."

I hugged her for an unusually long time. I knew she had spoken words I needed to hear.

Over the next few days, I pondered my daughter's advice. There are times when, to avoid jeopardizing a relationship with someone, we need to be tolerant of their decisions even when we disagree. We don't know all the circumstances influencing their decision. We certainly don't know everything in their heart. And if we expect them to be tolerant of the decisions we make, then we must do the same.

This experience reminded me of what Jesus taught the people gathered around Him on the mountain. "In everything do to others as you would have them do to you" (Matthew 7:12 NRSV). I've heard it often referred to as the Golden Rule. I like to think of it as having an accepting heart. Earlier in that chapter, Jesus cautions us not to judge others "or you too will be judged" (Matthew 7:1). And in fact, we are not judged for our sins because Jesus paid the penalty for us. His Easter gift allows us to stand before God without fear of judgement.

Who am I to judge my friend's decision? I wondered. Don't I expect her to be tolerant of my choices?

When I was sure my friend had returned home from her contract signing, I e-mailed her. "Did you have a good trip? How's your textbook progressing?"

Prayer

Help me, Lord God, to be tolerant when my friends don't make the decisions I think they should. Work in me an accepting heart so I can be supportive even when I don't understand their choices. Remind me of Your unconditional love and forgiveness amidst my own wrong choices. Keep me ever mindful of the judgment I am spared because of Christ's sacrifice for my sins. In Jesus' name I pray. Amen.

Journal Jottings

Describe a time when you tolerated a decision of someone close to you so it wouldn't jeopardize your relationship.

My Star

DOING THE IMPOSSIBLE

Jesus looked at them and said,
"With man this is impossible, but with
God all things are possible."
Matthew 19:26

After reading the long-awaited letter from the publishing company, I sat back in my office chair, bewildered. The amount of devotional material required and the timeline to produce it—create, write, and edit—seemed to me impossible.

My husband, after reading the letter, cautioned me not to be too quick with a negative response. "After all," he said, "you've always wanted to follow your star. Now that it's finally happened, don't pull back so fast."

I wasn't convinced. I gave him a "but-you-don't-understand look" and ended our conversation.

After turning out the lights that evening, I went to the Lord with the reservations and anxiety I'd shared with my husband. "You've shown me the star You want me to follow, Lord, but the journey You've shown me looks much too difficult." Before I could go on, I'd fallen asleep.

I put my response to my publisher out of my mind until the following Sunday in church when our pastor started preaching. From the beginning of his sermon, I sensed it had been penned for me.

He talked about the star the Wise Men saw and the thoughts of impossibility that might have run through their heads as they contemplated their journey. When I thought he'd reviewed every feeling of inadequacy the Wise Men could have ever had, he switched gears. "When the Wise Men pondered Who gave them their star—the One who made the impossible, possible—following it didn't seem so impossible after all." Our pastor explained, "God intercepted every misgiving the Wise Men might have had."

The congregation was well into its last hymn before I ended my musings. I'd been thinking about the star I'd seen, how impossible the journey seemed, and how inadequate I felt. Yet, when I considered the One who led me—the One who made all things possible, the One who was made incarnate to suffer and die for me—I knew He would empower me to begin my journey of writing with confidence. Encouraged, I knew God was leading me to write this book so I could encourage others in their journey of faith.

Just before our pastor pronounced the benediction, I poked my husband. "I think the answer I'll give the publishing company has changed." He looked at me quizzically. I whispered, "with God all things are possible."

Prayer

Lord Jesus, help me to follow my star, the star You have given me, not because I think I'm adequate for the journey, but because I know You will equip me for Your work. You make what seems impossible, possible. For You alone are my Star, the focus of my life's course. In Your name I pray. Amen.

Journal Jottings

Are you following the star Christ has given you, or do you think the journey's impossible? Tell why. Note: The book you hold was my star.

Four Cents Worth

TURNING AROUND A BAD DAY

*Therefore as we have opportunity, let us
do good to all people. Galatians 6:10*

I heard the January winds howling outside as the alarm
clock woke me from a deep sleep. Struggling out of bed,
not wanting to be late for my appointment, I asked my husband if he'd mind going with me. These sub-zero, pounding winds could trigger a winter storm anytime, and I was
nervous about driving into the city alone.

Usually more than willing to accommodate me in situations like this, that day proved to be an exception. My husband could not change his plans. He assured me the winds
would soon diminish; there were no storms forecast. Even
if one unexpectedly developed, he said, I had my cell
phone should I need help. Because of his unusual inflexi-
bility, I became grouchy. Convinced this day was going to
run anything but smoothly, I backed out of the garage in a
huff.

Twenty minutes later, I looked at my watch and noticed
I had just enough time before my appointment to drop off
a package to be shipped. At the register, the computer tal-
lied the amount I owed for mailing my parcel—$4.04.
Handing the clerk four one-dollar bills, I began rummaging
in my purse to find the remaining change. When I realized
I'd changed purses that morning and forgotten my coin
purse in my other bag, I gazed at the clerk in embarrassment. Now I'd have to lug around 96 cents worth of coins
in my purse the rest of the day.

"I just knew, as bad as my day was going, I'd do something foolish like this to put me in an even grouchier mood," I grumbled.

The clerk had already guessed what had happened. "I've done it quite often," she chuckled. Reaching for her purse, she pulled from her wallet four pennies, placing them in the cash register to finalize my transaction. "There's no use carrying around all that change all day," she smiled. She bid me a blessed day.

What had begun as an unusually grouchy day had quickly turned into a cheerful one because someone had sprinkled kindness upon me. If a simple act of kindness like this could turn *my* day around, I wondered what effect it could have on other people if I repaid the kindness.

After my appointment, I was given an opportunity to find out. I decided to stop at a familiar restaurant for some homemade soup. Irritated by the lunch crowd pestering her about the long wait, the hostess of the restaurant snapped at me, "Name? How many? Smoking or non-smoking?"

Not wanting to agitate her further but desiring to sprinkle kindness upon her instead, while I waited my turn in line I casually began asking her about her family. Soothed by our conversation, she calmly led me to a booth when the crowd thinned. I noticed a smile form across her face, for the first time, as she thanked me for showing a personal interest in her.

I couldn't help but think of the letter Paul wrote to the Colossians during his imprisonment in Rome. In chapter three he reminds his friends that since they are followers of Christ, they should model His life. "Therefore, as God's chosen people, holy and dearly loved, clothe yourselves with compassion, kindness, humility, gentleness, and patience. Bear with each other and forgive whatever grievances you may have against one another. Forgive as the Lord forgave you" (Colossians 3:12–13).

While driving home, the grouchies long since gone after having experienced an abnormally smooth, cheerful day, I pondered the reason for my bad mood and what effect kindness had had on me and the people I'd met that day.

It had a ripple effect, a thread that tied us together in our faith in Jesus as our Savior. *And to think it all started with four cents,* I smiled to myself.

Prayer

Merciful God, show me the ripple effect of kindness, and how it can turn a grouchy day into a cheerful one— not only when I'm touched by it, but also when You help me touch others with it. Remind me of the kindness You show me through Your grace and mercy, and through the gift of salvation in Your Son. In His name I pray, the Author of all kindness and goodness. Amen.

Journal Jottings

Instead of writing in your journal today, try sprinkling kindness upon someone else.

Not Home Yet

MINISTRY IN THE TWILIGHT YEARS

"As long as it is day, we must do the work
of Him who sent me. Night is coming,
when no one can work." John 9:4

She was in her mid-seventies, had lost her husband, and was showing increasing signs of mental confusion. For these reasons, and others, my aunt's family had decided to place her in a nursing home. She was far from pleased.

One autumn afternoon, shortly after my aunt had moved into the nursing home, I went to see her. To my surprise, I found her in her room curled up in her bed. No amount of convincing could get her up and moving.

"I'm here to die," she said matter-of-factly.

I attempted conversation about topics she'd always enjoyed. Knowing her love for flowers, I commented on the beauty of the potted mums in the courtyard. She showed no interest. Not even the sweet sponge cake I'd made for her stirred any emotion.

Finally, I crawled into bed with her and whispered emphatically, "Auntie, you aren't *home* yet." Before I left, I suggested she get out of bed. I reminded her of the people who needed her here, who needed to hear from her lips that Jesus loved them.

On the way home, although I'd tried to instill in my aunt a purpose for living, I thought about the hopelessness of her statement about being put in a nursing home to die. Sadly, I remembered how energetic she used to be, baking all sorts of cookies, then visiting endless hours with Mom and me over coffee in her home. Now she appeared fragile and spent.

That night while trying to fall asleep, I wrestled with my own thoughts. *Maybe I was wrong in telling her she wasn't home yet.*

The next morning, with both my aunt's remark and mine still on my mind, I took a walk down our farm lane. Gazing up into the gray overcast sky, I saw seven honking geese flying in perfect formation, homing their way south. By the sound of their honking, I imagined they longed to be home. "But we aren't home yet," they seemed to echo. And then, "Although we're old, we aren't dying. We're still flying our course, showing other geese the way home."

In that moment, I knew my message to my aunt hadn't been wrong. Christ would help me bring this message back to my aunt until she believed it too.

The next time I visited my aunt, I went straight to her room to give her the message Christ had given me through the homing geese. But I did not find my aunt in her room. As I was asking at the nurse's desk about her whereabouts, I recognized her slight frame down the hall, silhouetted in the late afternoon sun. She was pushing a woman in a wheelchair and chatting with her.

Walking down the hall, she beamed when she recognized me. "You were right, I'm not 'home' yet," she winked. She leaned closer and whispered about all the people here she'd found who needed to hear about Jesus.

Giving my aunt a gentle squeeze, I told her I'd come back another time. I didn't want to interfere with her rediscovered mission.

Prayer

Dearest Lord, thank You for the gift of long life. I know that even before I was born, You numbered my days on earth. Teach me to encourage people in their twilight years, give me the words to remind them that they are still a valuable part of Your kingdom on earth "while it is still day." Use me to spread the message of salvation through Jesus to all ages. In the Savior's name I pray. Amen.

Journal Jottings

Visit someone in a nursing home and share ideas for ways they can continue to live out Christ's purpose. Write what happens here.

Mysterious Bodyguards
Angels to Protect Us

"See, I am sending an angel ahead of
you to guard you along the way."
Exodus 23:20

To get our Sunday school class discussion rolling with our high schoolers, my husband and I asked, "Do you think God sends angels today to protect us like He did during biblical times?"

As expected, the youth offered a variety of responses. Some declared they didn't believe in angels. Others voiced, with strong conviction, they did. Then there were the "doubting Thomases" who said they'd believe if an angel was to step into their life and protect them. More than I cared to admit, I was in the ranks of the doubting Thomases.

After we'd let the discussion seesaw, we called a halt. Directing them to a couple of passages in Scripture, we studied how God intervened through His angels to protect His people.

The first passage we studied came from the book of Daniel. There, in the den of lions, God sent an angel to shut the lions' mouths and keep them from devouring His faithful servant, Daniel (Daniel 6:19–23). Another passage we explored was when an angel rescued Peter during the night from his jail cell and led him to safety (Acts 12:6–11).

"So what?" one teenager piped up. "How do these passages answer whether God sends angels to guard over us today?" Before we could answer, one of the girls in our group began telling a story that had happened to her Bible camp counselor while in college, capturing our attention like a mystery thriller.

Knowing it was late and the walk back to her dorm considerably long, the counselor whispered a quick prayer asking God to keep her safe as she left the library that night. About halfway to her dorm, a scruffy, weird-looking guy popped out directly in front of her. She gathered he'd hidden behind a tree. She thought the guy looked ready to assault her. To her astonishment, however, he never touched her. As quickly as he appeared, he disappeared back into the shadows.

The next morning, the counselor was awakened by her roommate. Her roomie, after watching the early morning news, informed her that a woman in her 20s had been raped and killed the night before. The crime took place in the area where she had been, at approximately the same time as she would have been there. A suspect had been apprehended. The police were asking anyone who had been in the vicinity during the time to help identify this man.

Skipping her morning classes, the counselor jumped on a bus that took her to the police headquarters. Approaching the desk sergeant, she explained who she was and the connection she might have had to the suspect. When asked whether or not she could recognize him, she responded with a firm "Yes."

After making a positive identification, she was allowed to ask the suspect why he had turned and run away from her the night before.

Dumbfounded, he mumbled, "Why wouldn't I? You had two muscular men standing right beside you, one on each side."

Shocked by his response, she retreated. She knew there hadn't been anyone escorting her the night before when she'd walked from the library back to her dorm. There could be only one explanation—they must have been angels.

After hearing this story from one of their peers, the class fell silent. For this doubting Thomas, I didn't need any more to convince me that God sends His guarding angels to us today.

Prayer

Loving Father, thank You for the many ways You guide me and keep me in Your care. Thank You especially for Your holy angels. Forgive me when I question their presence in my life. Strengthen my faith so I am confident and secure in Your promise to bring me safely into Your kingdom through the sacrifice of Your Son. In Christ's name I pray. Amen.

Journal Jottings

Tell of a time when you think God's angels watched over you or an acquaintance in a dangerous situation.

Gift Exchange
THE JOY OF GIVING

*Joseph and Mary took Him to Jerusalem
to present Him to the Lord ... and to
offer a sacrifice in keeping with what is
said in the Law of the Lord: "a pair of
doves or two young pigeons."*
Luke 2:22, 24

The weekend after Thanksgiving, my phone rang. From her shaky voice, I could tell my long-distance friend was upset. She didn't waste any time telling me why. At their family's Thanksgiving get-together a couple of days earlier, her sister requested the rest of the family have their Christmas gift exchange without them. Her husband had been laid off for three months and didn't know when or if he'd be recalled. She'd taken a part-time job, but earned barely enough to cover expenses. The kids were doing odd jobs just to earn pin money. Christmas gift-giving would only add another financial burden. Because her family couldn't afford to purchase gifts, they preferred not being in the gift exchange at all.

My friend was seeking advice whether to go ahead and have the gift exchange with just part of the family or drop it for this year. She didn't want anyone's feelings hurt. I gathered though, what my friend wanted most was another solution.

Her situation reminded me of a story that Gail, my dad's first hired man, had shared with me.

On Christmas Eve, left without a mother, Gail took the stocking his mother had knitted for him and hung it in its usual place. The Great Depression and his mother's untimely death had hit them hard that year. More than 40 years later, Gail still had tears in his eyes as he recalled that Christmas. His stocking had remained empty, his dad not knowing what to put in it as a symbol of his love.

I wondered if my friend's nieces and nephews would have a similar memory if they didn't exchange some kind of Christmas gift this year.

Another family came to mind. After Mary had delivered Jesus, when the time came for her purification, Joseph took his family, as required by Jewish law, to Jerusalem to offer sacrifices in the temple. Because Mary and Joseph couldn't give a lamb, they gave what they could. Their sacrifice to God was in the form of two young pigeons.

In the story of Mary and Joseph, I found the answer that eluded me before. I shared these thoughts with my friend. "Instead of excluding your sister's family from the gift exchange or dropping it entirely, why not propose that each family member give a form of their love this year." I offered what I thought were some creative, resourceful ideas: handmade stationery from paper they already had, baked goods from ingredients in the cupboard, or gift certificates for their time or expertise (car washing, gardening services, baby-sitting). "Actually, it's better than any gift you can buy," I said.

My friend thanked me for my time. She was eager to share these suggestions with her sister. "Maybe my sister's children will recall a memorable Christmas yet," my friend said as she hung up the phone.

That evening, with my long-distance friend's conversation fresh in my mind, I gazed at the drummer boy ornament on our tree and thought of the legend of the gift he gave to the Christ Child: love in the form of a melody he played on his drum. *Gifts come in many forms,* I thought, but the most precious gift comes in the form of our Savior. No matter what our circumstances are, we can always find ways to share the Gospel message of love and hope He brings us. Those are the threads of memories that make giving a real joy.

Prayer

Dearest Lord, sometimes circumstances may prevent me from giving the best material gifts. Help me, Lord, to remember that giving my best means sharing the Good News of salvation through the greatest gift—the birth of Your Son. Instill in me the joy of sharing that gift with people I love. I praise You and thank You for sending Jesus for me. In His holy name I pray. Amen.

Journal Jottings

Describe a gift you gave or received that cost little or nothing, but left you with beautiful memories.

Payroll Monotony
OVERCOMING JOB BOREDOM

He restores my soul. Psalm 23:3

To think of tackling payroll after already toiling eight hours at the desk on year-end reports left me frustrated.

"I'm sick of this monotony," I shouted to an empty house. If I'm not taking care of daily expenditures, I'm writing out weekly paychecks or figuring W-2s. Maybe, after 15 years straight of doing the same old thing day after day, I need a change, a job that's more uplifting. What does this job have to do with my faith anyway?

I stared crossly at the completed time cards on my desk vying for my attention. I jerked open the file drawer to find my payroll record book. Postponing my boring task, I decided to prepare a mug of tea.

"One of my favorite Christmas gifts," I warmly recalled, as I held up my designer mug to better study its design. Stamped around the mug in three different places was a picture of a school girl. She was standing in the open country with her satchel behind her back. Near the girl the designer had inscribed the words, "The Real Voyage Of Discovery Consists Not In Seeking New Landscapes But In Having New Eyes," Marcel Proust.

Maybe it'd be good for me, as I face this same landscape of weekly payroll drudgery, to see it with "new eyes," I thought. Instead of concentrating on how bored I was writing each paycheck, I started focusing on the people who would be receiving them.

The first payroll envelope I picked up belonged to the employee who had been with us the longest. He had lost his brother in an accident on one of our farms. While I wrote his paycheck, I prayed that Christ would bring him the healing, comfort, and peace he needed so his extended family could lean on him for emotional support like they'd done prior to his brother's death.

I opened the next envelope. This wage-earner headed a blended family. As I scrawled his paycheck, I asked the Lord to guide and bless him and his wife as they struggled through the delicate issues of parenting.

On down through the payroll list I moved, praying for each employee as I computed their pay.

One envelope reminded me of the many nights this worker had gone to technical school to position himself for a job less physically demanding. I petitioned Christ to grant him this dream. When I read the name on one job holder's envelope, I prayed for the baby he and his wife wanted to conceive. With another, I implored the Lord to soften the tragedy he too had experienced with his brother's death and make his life less stressful. When I turned over the next envelope, I lifted to Christ this person's longing to be married. Not as familiar with the newer employees, I simply asked the Lord to bless and care for them, whatever their needs were.

By the time I'd finished, something amazing had taken place within me. I'd been able to view the same landscape—the same repetitious, boring task—with "new eyes." Christ helped me focus on the people receiving these paychecks instead of the monotonous task of writing them. He restored my soul and helped me discover how my faith and job connected after all. All I needed were "new eyes," not a "new landscape."

Prayer

Sometimes when my job becomes monotonous, remind me, Lord God, to look with "new eyes" at the blessings You've given me. Help me discover creative ways for putting renewed interest back into my job—ways in which my work and my faith can be combined to further the work of Your kingdom and spread the Gospel message of salvation. Show me that even the things I think of as being mundane and unimportant can be done to Your glory. In Jesus' name I pray. Amen.

Journal Jottings

Tell what you can do to see your job through "new eyes."

Giving Myself Permission

ACCEPTING MYSELF

*I praise You because I am fearfully
and wonderfully made; Your works are
wonderful, I know that full well.*
Psalm 139:14

I was apprehensive as the orthotist wound the luke-
warm, slimy, white sheeting around my leg, forming a full-
length leg cast to use as a brace model. *How was I going to
keep accepting myself despite this illness?* It had been hard
enough accepting myself when I struggled with one brace.
Now I'd be contending with two.

My mind flashed back to a visit to a funeral home several years ago with a friend I'd known since childhood.

As my friend gazed into her mother's casket, I pulled up
a chair to sit beside her. Before long, we were talking quite
frankly with each other about the health challenges we
were facing due to our muscular illnesses. I asked how she
was able to accept herself being confined to a wheelchair.

With soft-spoken ease, she began sharing her journey
with me. She told me about the first time she knew she'd
be bound to a wheelchair, and how she shared this struggle of self-acceptance with her mother. Her mother was
already confined to a wheelchair due to cancer.

Simply, but quite convincingly, her mother said, "Giving
myself permission has made all the difference." Her mother didn't allow her illness to diminish how she accepted
herself as a person.

Ever since that day, my friend told me, she'd held tightly to her mother's words. "Despite my illness," my friend

emphasized, "I accept how I look on the outside simply by giving myself permission to do so." Just like her mother, she'd never allowed her disease to detract from who she was as a person.

"Even more important," she continued, "I accept who I am on the inside—a beautifully created and redeemed child of God. Why? Because God gives me permission to do so." In the larger scope of life, she stressed, that was what mattered the most.

I was brought back to the present as the orthotist painstakingly cut the cast away from my leg. My friend's strength and faith had strengthened me. My memory helped me realize that how I look makes no difference to who I am as a baptized and redeemed child of God. I was made perfect by Jesus' sacrifice.

I no longer dreaded wearing two full-length leg braces. I could accept myself now. The difference? God had equipped me to give myself permission.

Prayer

Lord God, despite how my illness makes me look on the outside, help me accept myself. Help me remember that what counts most is who You have made me to be on the inside. Keep me mindful that I am forever Your "wonderfully made," baptized, and redeemed child. In Jesus' name I pray. Amen.

Journal Jottings

Has an illness affected how you see yourself? Explain.

Two Enticing Sweaters
TAKING OR GIVING

*"For where your treasure is, there your
heart will be also." Matthew 6:21*

After getting our hair cut and eating lunch at our usual
spot, Mom and I decided to shop at our favorite boutique.
As we opened the door, the boutique's staff was unpack-
ing a shipment of sweaters. Like two kids in a candy store,
we started trying on the sweaters. I found a longer-length
tunic knitted in various shades of brown, black, and gray
that looked attractive on me. Mom found a shorter navy
cardigan that looked stunning on her.

"Are you going to buy yours?" Mom inquired.

"Of course," came my quick reply. "Aren't you?"

Mom looked thoughtfully at the sweater, as if she was
studying it. "I think I'll wait," Mom said quietly.

All the way home, I wondered how my mom could have
resisted buying the beautiful sweater she'd tried on.
Despite several stacks of neatly folded sweaters already in
my closet, I sure didn't have trouble convincing myself I
needed one more.

The next Sunday in church, when the breeze from the
ceiling fan blew open the check my parents had placed in
the offering plate, I accidently saw the amount. *So that's
why Mom didn't buy that sweater the other day,* I thought.
By taking less for herself, she had more to give to others.

Humbled, I realized that I had indulged in more than I
needed. Mom had chosen to give a greater portion back to
the Lord. I remembered Christ's words, "for where your
treasure is, there your heart will be also" (Matthew 6:21).

And I knew that my mother's example helped me put my treasures in perspective. Another thread had been woven.

Prayer

Gracious and giving Father, thank You for the many blessings of this life, for clothes to warm me and food to sustain me. All I have comes from You. Teach me, Lord, to be a good steward of these blessings, to take from life only what I *need*, rather than only what I want, so I'll have more to give back to You. In Jesus' name I pray. Amen.

Journal Jottings

What can you give up so you'll be able to give more generously to the Lord's work?

Compelled

CHANGING JOBS

The LORD ... said to Abram,
"Leave your country, your people, and
your father's household and go to the
land I will show you." Genesis 12:1

After praying our evening prayers together, our junior-higher popped a thought-provoking question, "Do you think God moves us, like He did Abraham, Moses, and Jesus' disciples, to new jobs?"

We gathered from the complexity of her question that she'd been discussing this topic in her Sunday school class. My husband, motioning me to answer, listened while I told her a story.

One morning before going to work, my sister's neighbor, Linda, was reading in Genesis how Abram was uprooted by God. As she was meditating on this Scripture passage, a compelling urge to leave her job enveloped her. "This must be the same feeling Abram had," she thought, "when God told him to leave his country, people, and home for an unknown place He would show him."

In the past, when she'd had this feeling, she'd paid little attention to it. This day, sensing more than usual that God would care for her needs, she could no longer ignore its urge.

Submitting to that trust, she telephoned her boss. Without another job firmly in place, without even as much as an interview lined up, she terminated her employment. This job, after all, had brought her only endless frustration.

This same afternoon, with her time all her own, Linda knocked on my sister's door to catch up on the latest news concerning my sister's pregnancy. After my sister told Linda about the complete bed rest her O.B. doctor had ordered for her, and Linda explained to my sister how she'd quit her job, Linda voiced the thought that was on both of their minds.

"Annie, I'm all yours. I'm convinced this is where Christ wants me for now, helping you get through your difficult pregnancy." Although Ann tried to convince Linda otherwise, suggesting she start looking for a new job immediately, Linda would have it no other way. "This is my new job, Annie," she said with conviction.

For the next two months, Linda did whatever jobs Ann needed done. Every day, she freshened up the house and cooked the main meal. Three times a week, she drove Ann's daughter to preschool. On scheduled days, she chauffeured Ann to her doctor's appointments. During this time, Ann and Linda prayed, asking God for a permanent job for Linda.

A couple of months after this routine began, as Linda was getting ready to go to Ann's home for the day's routine, the phone rang. A company for which Linda had always wanted to work was requesting she come in for an interview. A job to her liking and near her home had just opened up, one the company had not anticipated.

As Linda rushed over to tell Ann her good news and check on whether she could get along without her for a few hours while she interviewed, a neighbor stopped her. "Ann's husband tried to call you this morning, but your line was busy. He took Ann to the hospital this morning. She's already delivered a healthy full-term son!"

A few days after Ann brought her new son home with her, Linda knocked again on Ann's door with a batch of cookies she'd baked that morning. Besides these cookies, she was delivering some exciting news. The next morning was her first day at her new job, the one they had diligently prayed about.

The certainty of God's power in our lives is expressed in Jeremiah 29:11, "'For I know the plans I have for you,' declares the LORD, 'plans to prosper you and not to harm you, plans to give you hope and a future.'"

When I finished telling my daughter this story, I asked, "Now, what do you think? Does God, even today, oversee the course of life and nudge us to different places?"

"You bet He does," came her firm reply.

Prayer

Lord God, help me to listen and trust. Assure me that You are present in all aspects of my life, make the thread of hope in You present in all I do. Keep me firmly rooted in Your Word as I seek Your direction in my life. Strengthen my faith so that I, like Abraham, might hear Your call. Through Your Son, I pray. Amen.

Journal Jottings

Have you ever felt an urge to move in a different direction? Describe how the hand of God was in this whole process.

Like Clockwork

Do not be anxious about anything,
but in everything, by prayer and petition,
with thanksgiving, present your requests
to God. Philippians 4:6

Christmas Day was near. My sister, three hours away from the rest of our family, was hooked up to several in-home hospital monitors, near term with her second child. There was no way she and her family could make it home for Christmas. *So why not take Christmas to them?* The very thought of relocating Christmas dripped with work.

To successfully move Christmas, besides transporting all the food and gifts to my sister's home, numerous other details had to fall into place. Of utmost importance, all 10 of us had to be healthy so we didn't carry any illness with us. The Upper Midwest winter weather had to cooperate, making for clear roads. Perhaps the most difficult—all the chores on our farms had to be done that day by someone other than a family member.

Despite these roadblocks, I persuaded everyone to get behind the effort. The boost it would give our sister would be worth all our trouble.

Several days before the Christmas journey north, however, I began second-guessing my sanity. I started worrying if all the details would fit together as we'd planned. Before my worry crystallized into inaction, however, I talked with a friend who'd been through a similar situation the year before.

She commented, "I know exactly what you're going through. Last Christmas, due to our demanding schedules, in order to be with my parents on Christmas Day, everything had to run like clockwork."

She continued telling me how, shortly before Christmas Day, with her nerves wound tight, she picked up her daily devotional book. The day's text came from Philippians 4:6, reminding her to keep concern in its proper perspective; first by praying about it and then believing prayer would be answered. She decided, right then and there, to try it.

As she did, her worries diminished. Every detail worked out perfectly. Despite their cramped, six-hour drive in a day's time, they were able to spend Christmas Day with her parents.

That Christmas, after hearing my friend's story, I did exactly as she had done. Guess what? God smiled upon us and, just like her, no detail was left incomplete. As I could have anticipated, the spirits of my sister and her family were lifted. By the time we arrived home late Christmas Day night, every family member was glad they'd made the effort to go.

Prayer

I am always amazed, Lord God, how completely You take care of me. You know my every need and take care of every detail. Accept my prayers and nourish my faith. Strengthen my confidence in You, that every necessary thing will be provided. I pray in Jesus' name, whose life, death, and resurrection make all things possible. Amen.

Journal Jottings

Describe an event when every detail had to fit perfectly. How did you handle it? If faced with a similar event again, how will you turn to God to work it out?

Lay Readers

MOVING PAST EMBARRASSMENT

"Whatever you ask for in prayer
with faith, you will receive."
Matthew 21:22 NRSV

With much enthusiasm, my husband and I had agreed to be lay readers at my nephew's wedding. After the wedding rehearsal, though, our enthusiasm significantly paled. Whatever could have possibly gone wrong did.

My limited mobility had slowed the entire service as the wedding party waited patiently for us to walk up to the lectern. Once there, if we weren't losing our place, we were fumbling our words or forgetting to read with expression. Our final blunder came when we were returning to our pew. We stumbled into the musician's stand sending sheet music flying everywhere.

At the rehearsal dinner, I confided to my husband, "I bet the bride and groom wish they would have chosen anyone but us to be their lay readers." Giving me a peck on the cheek, he assured me that things would go better at the wedding.

The next morning, I was still troubled with visions of a repeat performance at the actual service. With my devotional book in my hand, I turned to the passage for the day. From Matthew 21:22, I read, "Whatever you ask for in prayer with faith, you will receive."

If only I had the faith right now to believe Christ would move us past the embarrassing moment we created for ourselves last night, I told myself. Folding my hands, I asked Christ not only to push the rattling memories of rehearsal away but to help us deliver with conviction and joy His words at the wedding service. Did I actually believe He could? I asked Him for one more thing, the faith to believe.

As the organ chords began resounding the jubilant strains of "Joyful, Joyful, We Adore Thee," I felt differently. I was no longer uptight or worried. I was actually looking forward to participating in the wedding service. *Faith had made the difference.*

As my niece finished the anthem, feeling calm inside, I reached for my husband's arm. Effortlessly, we walked to the lectern without noticeably interrupting the service. As we read, the people's faces reflected how the Holy Spirit was touching their hearts through His Word, bolstering their faith, and sprinkling them with gladness. We read without making a mistake. And we made our way back to our pew without stumbling.

Breathing a bit easier as the wedding service continued, I wondered how many times I had resisted Christ moving me past a difficult moment, tying a knot in the thread, knowing only He could make it right?

Prayer

Dearest Lord, You are so faithful to me, even when I rely on my own strength and not on You. Forgive me, Lord, for my shortcomings. Thank You for Your unlimited patience with me. Renew me and remind me of Your faithfulness, Lord, in all things, especially the promise of eternal life with You through Christ's death on the cross. Grant me the power to believe. In Jesus' name I pray. Amen.

Journal Jottings

Tell of a time in your life when you asked Christ to move you past an embarrassing incident, and trusted He would.

Bulging Suitcase

TOO MUCH STUFF

*"I will tear down my barns and build
bigger ones." Luke 12:18*

The day before I left for a conference in Florida, I located the largest suitcase we had and started packing.

"If the weather is sunny and warm," I speculated, "I'll need summer clothes." I rummaged through the packed closet where I stored summer clothes. I carefully folded and packed short-sleeved dresses and tops, skirts, and slacks.

"What if the weather is cool and rainy? None of these clothes will be warm enough." I poked through another closet. I folded a couple of wool slacks, a few turtlenecks, and a heavy sweater on top of the clothes I'd already packed.

"There's even a possibility the weather will be in-between." I packed some mid-weight clothes: some mock turtles, two pairs of gabardine slacks, and a denim dress.

By the time I'd finished packing, the suitcase bulged from both ends. Even with my husband's assistance, my suitcase refused to latch. Finally, after several attempts, by a stroke of luck, we got it to stay closed.

"How am I ever going to keep it shut while traveling?" I gave my husband a bewildered look. Leaving the room momentarily, he returned with a luggage strap he had found in the foyer closet.

"This safety strap should help you," he teased, as he secured the nylon strap around my suitcase. Even then, I had my doubts.

By the time I'd transferred planes and arrived at the baggage claim at the Florida airport where my parents met me, my doubts were confirmed. Coming rapidly down the luggage carousel, we spotted my open suitcase.

"Tell you what," my dad chuckled, "when you're done with your conference, we'll go to the mall and get you a replacement. You can call it an early birthday present. You have to promise me one thing though." I looked at him quizzically. "From now on, you'll carry a lighter suitcase by packing less stuff."

After the conference, my one free day before boarding the plane for home, the three of us drove to the mall. I can still see my dad grinning as he handed me the keys to my smaller, portable suitcase.

Journeying home, I thought about Dad's admonition. "You have to promise me you'll lighten up and carry less stuff." I started thinking of other spaces in my life that needed to be scaled down—areas cluttered with too much stuff. My jammed closets, tight schedules, and bulging suitcases were prime examples.

How much like the rich fool I have become, building ever bigger barns, preoccupied, and not leaving room for Christ to nourish my soul, I scolded myself (Luke 12:13–21). Perhaps it is time for me to lighten up, down-size, and simplify.

I had been so concerned about what I would wear, that I hadn't looked at the bigger picture of how I would manage traveling with the extra clothes. I had been greedy about my wardrobe.

Although I'm still a "clothes-a-holic," now I give away clothes to someone who needs them before I put a new item in my closet. To keep my calendar from overwhelming me, I'm learning to say no more often. And you've probably already guessed which suitcase I take whenever I go away.

With Christ's help I'm trying to focus my time on that which really counts—worship, His Word, and prayer. Admittedly, it's hard, and I still have much work ahead of me to scale down "my barns." To think that it all started with a bulging suitcase on the luggage carousel.

Prayer

Lord God, it's so easy for me to pack my life with too many activities and possessions. Refocus me through worship, Your Word, and the gifts of Your grace that I might avoid building bigger barns. Help me to lighten up, scale back, and simplify my life so I am better prepared to serve You. In Jesus' name I pray. Amen.

Journal Jottings

Is there any place where you feel you need to downsize and simplify your life?

A Perfect Heart

He brought her to the man. Genesis 2:22

Do you remember when you were in elementary school and made hearts from construction paper for Valentine's Day? I recall sitting in my second grade classroom. Art class was starting. After handing me a clean sheet of red construction paper, my teacher showed me how to fold it, draw on it, cut it, and open it so half of a heart magically became a whole one. After folding my paper in half and drawing half of a heart on it, I cut it out. When I unfolded it, my heart was just like my teacher's.

I was not satisfied with one heart, however. I wanted to make two hearts exactly alike. But I cut away too much on my second heart. It lost its shape and didn't match the first one. I had to start over.

For many years of my marriage, I did this same thing. I tried so hard to make my husband and me exactly alike. In reality, we were anything but alike. I liked a neat, orderly closet. It didn't bother my husband if his sweaters weren't stacked neatly in rows. He enjoyed reading the paper after our evening meal; I savored talking. Being indoors writing was my preference; his was being outdoors farming. We were quite different.

Sadly, I began noting our differences as his imperfections. He in turn began noting mine. I reasoned he should change and become more like me. Naturally he thought I should try to be more like him. In our subtle and not so subtle ways, we started working to change each other. But neither of us was willing to change. In the course of this journey, we traveled down some unpleasant paths, but God led us to discover an important truth.

Nothing I could do on my own made our hearts perfectly fit together. When we quit trying to change the other, quit trying to cut away our differences and imperfections, quit trying to make us exactly like the other, we began to accept the reality that we were different and imperfect.

Our marriage, in the presence of God, joined our imperfect hearts together as one heart. Now I can rejoice in our differences and the surprising richness those differences bring to our life as a couple united in holy matrimony. Accepting this, we're better able, with help of the Holy Spirit, to bring out the best in each other, blessing one another through our love and through His presence in our lives together. Through our union, we can live as witnesses to Jesus' perfect heart and His gift of perfect love for each of us.

Prayer

Lord God, I give You thanks for the gift of Christian marriage which You designed. Help me learn to accept and respect our differences. Show me how You can use these differences to bring out the best in us and in each other. And remind me of the perfect love that was made possible through the marriage feast of the Lamb. Through the blood of Your Son, our Savior, bless our marriage. Amen.

Journal Jottings

God created our differences to bless our lives together in Him. Make a list of the differences you bring to your marriage, then write a prayer of thanks for your spouse.

Runaway Grocery List

She can laugh at the days to come.
Proverbs 31:25

Opening every cupboard door in our kitchen, I made a list of all the groceries we'd need for the upcoming weekend. Waves of company were coming from both sides of our family. Except for this day, after my brace appointment, there'd be no other time to make the 25-mile trip for groceries. As I scurried off to shove some clothes in the dryer, I laid my grocery list down.

I checked the answering machine, jotted down some telephone messages, and left a note for my daughter on the desk. By the time I was ready to leave, I couldn't find my grocery list anywhere. While my husband showered and dressed, I asked him if he'd seen the list. Of course he hadn't. He'd just come in from work.

Frantically, I retraced my steps. No grocery list was to be found. I sputtered, "I wonder where it could have runaway to?"

My husband, getting impatient, offered to sift through the two stuffed garbage sacks at the back door. Maybe, by mistake, the grocery list had fallen into one of them. No list turned up. I even looked in the dryer. I thought maybe I'd dropped it in with a load of clothes. I still came up short.

Finally, while my husband waited for me to hastily scribble another grocery list, I moaned, "Why am I more forgetful now than usual?"

How well my husband knew the times recently when my forgetfulness had peaked. Many times I'd taken down an important number to call, then I couldn't remember where I'd put it. Or I'd gone from one end of the house to the other without remembering what I was looking for. As to the reason for such behavior, my husband kept still. I blamed it on midlife.

By nightfall, even after we'd bought our groceries and put them away, I still had no clue as to where my original grocery list was.

The next morning, while we were eating breakfast, my eyes fell on the note I'd hastily left on the desk yesterday for our daughter. "You don't suppose I left my grocery list under that note?" I asked. Sure enough, on the back of the note was the lost grocery list. At that moment, I could have cried over how forgetful I'd been, but I laughed instead.

I was reminded of the time Jesus visited Martha and Mary. Martha was caught up in making everything perfect for Christ's visit. Mary dropped everything she was doing and sat at His feet to listen to Him. Like Martha, I want everything to be perfect for my guests. I get caught up in the preparations. And I sometimes forget that the important thing about their visit is the joy we share in fellowship.

This episode taught me that I need to slow down and pay closer attention to what I am doing. Far more important, though, I need to relax and appreciate what is important about my relationships. As the first wave of company pulled into our driveway, instead of being anxious, I could now "laugh at the days to come" (Proverbs 31:25). It felt good.

Prayer

Merciful God, help me to be easy on myself when I'm forgetful. Teach me, rather than sputtering and crying, to laugh over my memory lapses. Remind me to slow down and focus on the daily tasks that are important, so I am better prepared to focus on the fulfillment of Your promises through Christ Jesus. In His name I pray. Amen.

Journal Jottings

Describe a time when, because of your forgetfulness, you ended up laughing at yourself and life.

No One Else

SACRIFICING MY COMFORT

And the Spirit immediately
drove him out into the wilderness.
Mark 1:12 NRSV

After he had been hacking and coughing from an upper respiratory infection for more than a week, I had finally convinced my husband he should have a doctor examine him. I hadn't been able to persuade him, though, to give up his plans to head up the crew that was loading turkeys for market that sub-zero night.

When he returned from his visit with the doctor, although she'd instructed him to stay out of the cold and get plenty of rest, he couldn't get outside fast enough. He said he had to get equipment set up for the work to be done.

I knew full well about the gut-grinding, dusty, back-breaking process of loading: chasing the turkeys into a holding pen, lifting them individually onto a conveyor, and manually placing them in cages on the truck. It was physically demanding for the most fit person, let alone one who was ill.

After setting up the loader, my husband shuffled to the house, showing signs of exhaustion, his face etched with fatigue and pain. I joined him while he gulped a mug of tea loaded with honey. "Why do you want to take this toll on your health just to be out there with your loading crew today?" I asked him.

He snapped back, "If I expect my crew to be out there in these frigid conditions, I'm going to be there with them.

There's a job to be done. It doesn't matter how I'm feeling. I'm not going to be comfortable while they're not." The conversation ended abruptly.

Later in the day, I looked out my iced windowpane to the barely visible building where I knew my husband was helping load the birds. "Why hadn't I been able to convince him to let his loading crew handle the work this time?" I wondered. "Why was he willing to sacrifice his health for others?"

At that moment, an insight into my husband's behavior dawned on me. I realized that he felt there was no one else who could do this job at this time. He worked side by side with the loading crew, despite his illness, because he recognized his responsibility as their leader. He was modeling Christ-like servant leadership.

Christ was willing to sacrifice for us, His motley crew members, at a far greater expense than His health—that of His own life. No one else could do it. There was no one else who could take Christ's place. No one else could sacrifice His most perfect world and enter this wilderness of hardships and dangers just to be sin for us. No one else could do this job—save this motley crew from our sins.

Prayer

Dearest Savior, there was no one else who could save me from this wilderness of trouble and sin. You came to rescue me, although it cost You Your life. Teach me how to serve others, despite discomfort or expense. Lead me to Your Word and send Your Holy Spirit to work in me a desire to model Your servant leadership. In Your name I pray. Amen.

Journal Jottings

Describe a time when you had to forego your own comfort for others.

Family Time

LEARNING TO SHARE MY TIME

"Who are my mother and my brothers?"
He asked. Mark 3:33

Everyone wanted a chunk of my family's time lately, so much so, we'd barely had any time alone with one another. Since nothing had been penciled in on the calendar for the Sunday afternoon following New Year's, it seemed the perfect time to have my family all to myself. No one would be crowding in on us or vying for our attention.

How I anticipated these brief hours. I had it all planned. After church, following a simple lunch, we'd take down the Christmas tree. Sipping hot chocolate, we'd play a game of "Gestures" and reminisce about the past Christmas. No one was going to intrude on our time together. Right?

Shortly after I revealed my plan to my husband and daughter, the high school youth from our Sunday school class announced that the gospel rock group we'd promised to take them to hear was making a one-time appearance in our area. The date coincided with the afternoon I'd planned for our family.

After we dismissed our class, I grumbled to my husband, "Why can't people leave us alone, at least this one afternoon, so we can have some family time together?" He remained quiet.

Less than 24 hours before we were scheduled to take our young people to this concert, I came down with a serious throat infection. Knowing this would keep me home that day, forcing me to take down the Christmas tree alone, I fumed all the more.

"So much for the family time I'd planned," I said as I washed the Sunday dinner dishes all by myself while my daughter and husband got ready for the concert.

Hearing my complaints, which were more audible than I'd thought, my husband slipped into the kitchen. Hugging me, he said, "Sometimes when people infringe on our family time, we need to realize that our true family stretches way beyond these four cloistered walls."

Later, as I removed the ornaments from the tree, the words my husband had said before leaving kept reclaiming my attention. Focusing on these words, I recalled a scene from Jesus' life.

Scripture records that one day Mary went with Jesus' brothers to the place where Jesus was teaching. She sent word to Jesus that his mother and brothers wanted to see Him. Jesus sent back His reply. "'Who are my mother and my brothers?' He asked. … 'Whoever does God's will is my brother and sister and mother'" (Mark 3:33–35).

I reflected how, even when Jesus knew his family desired time with Him, He chose to remain with the crowds. He considered them just as much His family as those He'd grown up with. He knew how important it was to communicate that we are all members of the same family, children of the same heavenly Father.

Seeing the last ornament jiggling on the tree, my thoughts returned to my family. I thought, "When I want my family all to myself, I need to remember what it means to be a baptized member of God's family. My true family lies beyond these four protective walls."

Hearing the garage door open told me my daughter and husband were home from the concert. With bubbling enthusiasm, she told me about their awesome experience. "A few of the kids who normally don't get involved as much as we do really enjoyed the concert, Mom. By the time the group sang their last number, it seemed we were ..." she stopped her sentence in mid-air.

I finished her sentence for her, "one big, happy family."

Prayer

Lord Jesus, when it seems that everyone wants a chunk of my family's time and we don't have time to be alone with one another anymore, remind me that my true family stretches much farther than those I grew up with or those I may be nurturing now. Keep me aware that through Baptism, we are all one family, Your children in faith. In Your name I pray. Amen.

Journal Jottings

List the people you consider to be your family. Pray for them by name.

A Mouse in Our House

*But immediately Jesus spoke to them and
said, "Take heart, it is I; do not be
afraid." Matthew 14:27 NRSV*

My husband found me in a strange place—perched awkwardly on a window ledge—one noon when he walked into the kitchen for lunch. With a blush, I announced, "There's a mouse in our house." Before he had time to say another word, I explained with much embarrassment, "I climbed up here so it wouldn't scamper over me. I don't know why I let a little mouse scare me so much."

By the time he'd found the traps and baited them, our lunch was cold. We ate in silence.

After he left, I panicked whenever I heard a noise in our house. I decided the best way to tackle my fear was to barricade myself in the library for the afternoon, hoping the mouse wouldn't find me there. For reinforcement against this little critter, I even jammed bath towels under the door. But as much as I tried to focus on my work, I was distracted by every creak and groan. I kept watching the towels to see if they were moving.

Still a bit embarrassed about my fear, I thought of another time in my life when I'd been even more nervous than this. It happened a few years ago when my doctor detected an unusual spot on my mammogram. I was petrified, thinking I might have breast cancer. A biopsy revealed the spot was benign, but the episode left me apprehensive.

As I was considering how fearful ordinary things like mousetraps and mammograms made me, I recalled when

Jesus' disciple Peter became paralyzed with immobilizing fear.

Early one morning, Jesus came walking on the sea toward His disciples. He assured them who He was. Peter, wanting to be convinced, declared, "Lord, if it's You, tell me to come to You on the water" (Matthew 14:28). He told Peter to come. Peter obeyed.

Peter was safe walking on the water as long as he kept his eyes and his thoughts focused on Jesus. The minute he became distracted by the wind and water—distracted by his fear—he began to sink.

Jesus can help me stay focused on Him instead of my fears, I told myself, He'll give me strength to control my fear, strength to walk above the waters of my fear. My fears will then no longer immobilize me.

Because of my afternoon's musings, my fears had eased even before I heard the mouse trap snap.

Prayer

Dear Jesus, forgive my weakness and fears, and help me to center my heart and mind on You. Assure me that no matter what confronts me, You will give me strength to walk above the waters of my fear. When I fail and am distracted by the cause of my anxieties, reach out for me as You did with Peter. As You continue to reach out to me through Your body and blood, remind me, Lord, that because You are my salvation and my stronghold, I have nothing to fear. In Your name. Amen.

Journal Jottings

Tell how God has helped you control a fear. Write a prayer that reminds you of the source of your strength.

Wasted Day

Be careful then how you live,
not as unwise people but as wise,
making the most of the time.
Ephesians 5:15–16 NRSV

I felt so refreshed yesterday because I selfishly wasted the entire day on myself. Yes, you read this sentence right. How dare say I spent the whole day on myself?

For nearly 365 days of the year, as a woman, wife, and mother, I'm making sure life flows smoothly, especially for my family.

I'm making sure I get to most, if not all, of my daughter's school activities.

I'm making sure I'm doing all that's expected of me to keep our financial records in good order so our farming business runs smoothly.

I'm making sure all the meals are planned and prepared, the clothes laundered, the dishes promptly washed, and the house picked up.

I'm making sure my husband and daughter get enough hugs.

I'm making sure my teenager gets transported to her private piano and voice lessons once a week.

I'm making sure our family has quality devotional time together.

I'm making sure our personal bills are paid and our monthly budget maintained.

I'm making sure I'm there for my teenage daughter when she needs me, while at the same time respecting her space.

I'm making sure everyone in my family knows where they're supposed to be and when.

I'm making sure our correspondence is answered promptly.

I'm making sure my writing time doesn't intrude on my other responsibilities.

I'm making worship a priority so the seeds of faith can continue to be planted. I'm making time for co-teaching Sunday school with my husband every Sunday morning.

I'm making sure I'm doing everything I promised to do whether in church, club, or the committees I serve on.

I strive to give wherever I'm needed most: as a wife, mother, nurse, counselor, cook, cleaner, advocate, banker, mediator, writer, etc. By the time I've taken care of everybody else's needs, there's hardly any time left to take care of my own.

Jesus and His disciples faced this same problem during their ministry on earth. His solution? It was really quite simple. He instructed them to "'come with Me ... and get some rest'" (Mark 6:31). Even God rested after He worked to create the earth and all living things on it (Genesis 2:2).

Yesterday, hearing His words anew, I accepted His gift of rest. I withdrew from my normal, hectic routine and spent the whole day doing something I seldom do. I nurtured myself, engaging in those activities I enjoy most.

To get my day started, I was pampered at the hair salon. Following my spoiling there, I ate a leisurely lunch at my favorite tea room. During the afternoon, I shopped, uninterrupted, at a fancy boutique. I sipped a strawberry Italian soda in the bookstore cafe while browsing through the pages of a new book. Finally, I capped the day off by listening to my favorite music on the drive home.

By the time I arrived home and met my family, I felt relaxed, refreshed, and energized.

As women, wives, and mothers, so much of our time is spent satisfying the needs of others. Sometimes "making the most of your time," as Ephesians 5:16 (NRSV) points out, simply means spending a day, without guilt, nurturing ourselves. That way, we can more effectively live for God and give back to others. It's another sign of His gracious love to us.

Prayer

Thank You, Lord God, for the gift of a day of rest and relaxation—one that strengthens and stimulates me so I can return to my busy life and effectively give back to those You've entrusted to my care. Refresh me and renew me so I can be a better witness to Your love and promise of salvation. In Jesus' name I pray. Amen.

Journal Jottings

Instead of writing in your journal today, spend the time on yourself, doing what you enjoy most.

"Hello, Jen?"

Train a child in the way he should go.
Proverbs 22:6

My nephew and his wife phoned us. "Want to go with us to see 'Phantom of the Opera'?" they asked; they had two extra tickets for the matinee. We eagerly accepted their invitation.

When I found out our daughter didn't have plans for that day, I tried to get her a ticket too. Unfortunately, the performance was sold out. "If only I'd known earlier," I said in disappointment.

When I told my daughter I wasn't able to get her a ticket, she was disheartened. I suggested she invite a friend over to spend that time with her. She gave me a noncommittal shrug.

Feeling guilty, I tried to think of something else she might do that day. I phoned her cousin. He had already made plans. I wondered if her cousin in college would be willing to come home for the weekend. When I phoned her, she had a choir rehearsal she couldn't miss. I almost called my brother; then remembered they were on a trip and wouldn't be home either.

The next day, while still trying to make plans for my daughter, I ran into a friend who had raised two teenagers himself. When I told him about my situation, he advised me to start letting my daughter make some of her own decisions.

He explained, "If you do, she'll be a lot happier because she'll learn to function independently. If you don't, she'll become a clone of you instead of her own person." He went on to say that the hardest thing he went through while parenting his teenagers was stepping back and trusting; watching them make their own decisions and mistakes. "But that's how they discovered who they were," he said.

His words hit home. I knew that God would always keep our daughter in His care. But stepping back and trusting that she would be okay without my constant guidance was difficult. Perhaps it was because I wasn't ready to let go, even just this little bit. Perhaps it was because I wasn't sure if I had prepared her enough. Or perhaps it was because I needed faith that God had helped my husband and me to train her so she would be ready to make some decisions on her own.

I decided to take our friend's advice and give my teenage daughter freedom in making some of her own decisions. When I reached home, I asked my daughter if she'd made any plans yet. She still hadn't.

"Maybe you should make your own plans this time," I suggested, then added, "I'll stay out of them. I trust your good judgment."

Surprised at my withdrawal, she picked up the portable phone and headed for her bedroom. "Hello, Jen?" I caught words like "pizza, videos, and computer" from their conversation.

Jen spent the afternoon with our daughter. When we arrived home, our daughter cheerfully greeted us. "Jen and I are going to meet each other at the basketball game Friday night."

We nodded, smiling. Our friend's advice was well received.

Prayer

Father God, my daughter is a beautiful blessing to me. Thank You for entrusting her to my care. Remind me that You have a unique plan for her life, a plan that is not a clone of my own life. Take away my fear. Help me trust that You will bless my best efforts to help her learn to make good choices. Give me wisdom to know when to step back and let her make decisions for herself. And send Your Holy Spirit to strengthen her faith and mine in Your Son as our Savior. In Jesus' name. Amen.

Journal Jottings

What happened when you let your teen make a decision on his or her own without your guidance? If you don't have a teen, describe a time when your mother let you make your own choices.

Warm Restaurant ...
Cold Van

SHARING MY BLESSINGS

"At his gate was laid a beggar named Lazarus." Luke 16:20

Ever since my nephew married, my husband, daughter, and I have been taking him and his wife out to dinner for his birthday. One year near his special day, I called him to make plans to meet him and his wife for dinner at his favorite restaurant the next Saturday night at 6:00. I told him if there were any changes, I'd call him back.

After school that day, when I mentioned our plans to our daughter, her face turned long. "That's the night I'm scheduled to feed the homeless with our church's youth group." We'd forgotten. Since we couldn't find another night that week when all three of us were free, my husband and I decided to keep our original plan.

That Saturday night, as the four of us were served immense portions of scrumptious food in a warm restaurant, I couldn't help but think of our daughter. Most likely, she was bundled against the weather, serving small amounts of donated food to the homeless out of a cold van. I recalled the parable Christ told to His disciples about the rich man and Lazarus.

While the rich man dined on the very best life offered, beneath his table sat a poor, diseased man named Lazarus. Lazarus continually begged the rich man to throw him some scraps from his overflowing table, but the rich man kept it all for himself. When at last Lazarus and the rich man died, the rich man went to hell and Lazarus went to heaven. The rich man begged for relief, but was told that since he had trusted in his wealth on earth as his god, there would be no hope of relief.

When I looked at our table laden with fine food and thought of the hungry homeless our daughter was feeding, the magnitude of the story hit me. *I was the rich man.* I found myself asking, *why is life so incredibly unbalanced?* In that moment, Christ led me to an answer.

"What if you would share with those who have nothing?" His voice seemed to guide. I answered back, "Then I would be as You redeemed me to be."

Prayer

Most gracious Lord Jesus, make me aware of how richly You have blessed me with plenty of food and a warm home. I indeed have barns overflowing. Guide me to share with those who are less fortunate, so no one lacks in the bounty which You have given. Give me the words to share with them the Good News of salvation through faith so they might be fed with the Bread of Life. In You, who provides for my every need. Amen.

Journal Jottings

Tell how you can share the blessings God has lavished upon you.

Prompted

We always thank God the Father of our
Lord Jesus Christ ... because we have
heard of your faith in Christ Jesus.
Colossians 1:3–4

My aunt and her traveling companion were spending a few days with my parents. My parents invited us to have dinner with them so we could meet my aunt's friend. We'd readily accepted their kind invitation.

Since dinner wasn't quite ready and Mom wanted to work alone in the kitchen, I walked into the living room where Dad was in his recliner reading the Sunday paper. My aunt's friend was moving around the room studying the many antiques in my parents' home. I started telling her the history of each one.

My dad interrupted us with a joke, "Having lived in this same house all my life, I consider myself an antique."

It didn't take my aunt's friend long to pick up on this quip, recounting her father's history. "My dad, still living at the ripe age of 84, grew up in a mining town in West Virginia." We listened intently as she told how her daddy was raised in the lifestyle of Daniel Boone. As she talked, I noticed she covered many details, all but one. She never mentioned anything about his faith. I wondered if Dad had picked up on this as I had. If so, would he say anything about it to someone he had only just met?

Dad, in his mild-mannered way, continued the conversation. He recalled a visit he'd had with a neighbor of his shortly before this neighbor died. This neighbor had shared with him the three gifts he intended to leave his children.

The first gift was a love for the land. Dad added that everyone should have a kinship with the soil. The second gift, Dad explained, was the opportunity to achieve an education. Dad pointed out that an education taught a person how to think and appreciate life from many perspectives.

"Last ..." there was a long silence. I already knew what Dad was thinking.

But how would he talk about his faith without offending her, not certain what her faith was? I wondered.

"Last, but what I consider to be the most important, my neighbor desired to encourage his children in their love for the Lord." Dad then went on to summarize his own faith journey. He ended the conversation by softly saying, "My neighbor's list just isn't too bad."

At that moment, Mother called us for dinner.

Alone in my recliner back home, I reflected on two things that had happened that day. We didn't know what this woman's relationship with God might have been, but my dad didn't hesitate to share his faith with her. Second, he witnessed his faith simply, without pushing or parading it. By retelling a conversation about the important matters of life, Dad had graciously shared with a person he'd just met what Christ meant to him.

Simply offering the Good News to others without offending them is a good model for my own life, I thought.

Prayer

Lord God, when an opportunity arises for me to share my faith with others, give me courage to react and the words to say. Teach me how to witness to Your mercy and grace without pushing or offending. Open their hearts through the power of the Holy Spirit. Help me live my life as a reflection of Your love and forgiveness in Christ. In Jesus' name I pray. Amen.

Journal Jottings

Tell of a time when you shared your faith in a gracious, non-threatening manner.

Sea Turtle

*"I have called you by name, you are
mine." Isaiah 43:1 RSV*

I had been coming to this coast in Florida for 15 years, each time to be rejuvenated. This time, however, I needed more than rejuvenation. I needed healing.

I longed for healing from physical pain. Throughout the winter months in the Midwest, I'd battled a chronic virus that I hoped rest and lots of sunshine would cure. I yearned also for healing from emotional anguish. My aunt, who was close to me, was dying. Soon I wouldn't have her praying presence bolstering my confidence.

I knew that I also needed healing in my faith life. For several months I'd worked on this book, trying to open my soul to others so they might be nurtured in their faith walk. And there were times that I struggled, crowding Christ out of my life. I craved spiritual renewal.

One afternoon during our visit, while walking along the ocean with my husband, I compared myself to its vastness. I felt insignificant. *With so many people needing His attention, why would God even bother with taking care of my needs, as puny as they are? Other people have far more pressing concerns for Him to attend to,* I thought. We moved along the water's edge, covering other people's footprints with each step.

We stopped by a rock to rest and noticed a commotion. Not far from us, a crowd gathered around two robust men who were bent down. When we reached the crowd, we saw that the men, their hands protected with thick gloves, were taking care of a sea turtle. A bystander, who had been watching the whole thing, filled us in on the details.

A sea turtle, approximately 24 inches in diameter and 80 pounds in weight, had come ashore. The turtle's algae-covered shell and the fact that it had come ashore a month too early, the man told us, meant that the creature was probably sick. A sea turtle's natural migration from the water to lay their eggs in the sandy ocean beach occurred later in the spring.

The bystander continued telling us what would happen next to the sea turtle. Having received permission to take it from its natural environment, these men would periodically splash sea water on its encrusted body. Then, they'd wrap the turtle in towels, haul it up the beach's boardwalk, and place it in a bath tub in a house belonging to a trainer from Sea World. From there it would be transported to Sea World in Orlando where it would stay until it was healthy enough to return to its natural environment.

About an hour later, sprawled in our beach chairs, we watched as the two men hauled the sea turtle up the boardwalk. As we watched, I couldn't help but think of the words Jesus spoke in Matthew 6, telling His listeners to look at the birds of the air and the flowers of the field. They are not as valuable to God as we are, His precious children, yet our heavenly Father takes care of their needs. Jesus told His followers not to worry, that God would care for their needs too (Matthew 6:25–34).

As we continued to watch the sea turtle's removal from the beach, I realized if God, my Creator, would care for the needs of one animal like this sea turtle, then He will take care of my concerns too. I am much more valuable to Him than a sea turtle. When God made me His child through Holy Baptism, He promised that He would always care for my needs. I can't do anything to earn God's care; I receive it through His Word and sacraments. Just like that sea turtle can't do anything to earn the care it receives to restore it to health.

I had come to the sea for physical healing and emotional rejuvenation. I received that, along with the reassurance of His splash of grace.

Prayer

Sometimes, Creator God, I feel insignificant, like my life, in the great scheme of things, really doesn't matter. Then a splash of Your grace washes over me, reminding me how much You care for me—Your called and redeemed child. Thank You for sending Your Son to wash away my sins, for making a place for me in Your kingdom. And thank You for restoring my faith through the gift of Your promises to me. In Christ's sustaining name I pray. Amen.

Journal Jottings

Describe a time when the Holy Spirit worked in your life to restore your faith in God's love for you.

Two Different Reactions

"Give to everyone who asks you."
Luke 6:30

Scene One: A sidewalk in New Orleans, Louisiana. My daughter walked through one of the poorest sections of New Orleans when she went from the Superdome to her hotel room. One afternoon, as she neared her hotel, she noticed a man with filthy hair and scraggly beard in a dilapidated wheelchair. He held an equally filthy cup. His intentions were scrawled on a piece of cardboard: "Donations for a new wheelchair."

She immediately thought of the extra cash stashed in her fanny pack. *Maybe I should give him some money.* But she wondered if he might spend the money on something other than a wheelchair—maybe even something she didn't approve of. So she walked right past him, avoiding eye contact.

Scene Two: A path in Cocoa Beach, Florida. Walking to the grocery store one morning, my mother and father came upon a young, obviously homeless man sitting on a park bench. Glancing at him, Dad thought he looked hungry.

A half hour later, after buying enough provisions to last a week, they headed home the same way they'd come. When Dad saw the man in another area of the park holding a discarded piece of pizza, he approached him. After listening to his story, Dad reached into his sack and pulled out a loaf of fresh bread. Then, fiddling in his pocket for some change, he offered that to him also.

"Now I can buy something good to eat," the man said and walked off in the direction of the grocery store.

When Mom questioned Dad's generosity and whether this man had told the truth, he answered, "Whether I believed his story isn't important. What is important is that I gave to him."

Jesus makes it clear that when we give to those who are in need, we also give to Him. "'I tell you the truth, whatever you did for one of the least of these brothers of mine, you did for Me'" (Matthew 25:40). My father knew that. My daughter let her anxiety about the sins of this world sway her. I wondered what I would have done had I been there.

Prayer

Lord Jesus, when I'm approached by someone in need, help me follow my father's example and give as I am able. Help me teach my daughter to give generously to others. Remind me that I am a beggar too, always in need of Your grace. Open my heart as the Holy Spirit works in me to Your glory. In Your name. Amen.

Journal Jottings

Tell how you responded the last time you saw someone in need.

Happy Face Umbrella

IGNORING IMITATIONS

I will guide you with My eye.
Psalm 32:8 NKJV

While I was shopping one day, I got caught in a downpour. Soon I noticed umbrellas in all sizes and colors sprouting up around me. But none of them was a jumbo neon yellow umbrella with a hand-painted happy face on the outside, like the one my daughter often talks about.

My daughter's church group, along with several thousand others, converged on New Orleans one summer to attend a national youth gathering at the Superdome. With 39,000 people in the same place, her group decided they needed a visual cue to help them stay together.

One enterprising guy volunteered, "I have a huge yellow umbrella. We could take a black marker and draw a happy face on it."

The rest of the group enthusiastically agreed. Within minutes, his umbrella looked like a gigantic smiley face.

As long as their group stayed within sight of the one-of-a-kind umbrella, they remained safely together. No one wandered off. In the mass of moving humanity, they were always guided safely.

By midweek, however, as other groups caught on to this clever idea, yellow umbrellas with happy faces began popping up all over the Superdome. Among the imitations, it became increasingly harder for their group to distinguish their original one. With so many similar umbrellas, their group realized that for them to make it safely back to their hotel, they couldn't get diverted by look-a-likes. It wasn't enough to just recognize their umbrella, they would have to stay under it as well. This proved to be no easy task.

After the downpour, I watched the umbrellas snap shut one by one, and I thought how my daughter's umbrella experience at the youth gathering was a lot like being a Christian today.

If I don't stay under the safety of Christ, if I follow look-a-likes—other gods that pop up in my path—I'll never find my way home. To distinguish the one true God from the multitude of imitations, I need to stay close to Him through His Word and Holy Meal. By joining other believers under Christ's umbrella, I am protected by His promise to guide me with His watchful eye (Psalm 32:8 NKJV) and lead me safely home. He's my original happy-face umbrella.

Prayer

Help me to stay under Your happy face umbrella, Lord Jesus, and not be lured into following imitations. It's the only way I can be assured I'll be led safely home. I rejoice in Your grace and faithful promise to bring me life ever-lasting. In Your name I pray. Amen.

Journal Jottings

Has your faith ever been challenged by an imitation of Christ? Describe your experience and how the Holy Spirit strengthened your belief in Jesus as your Savior.

Time Capsule

"As for me and my household,
we will serve the LORD." Joshua 24:15

One day in May, our study club visited Hotel Pattee, a historic landmark in Perry, Iowa. This hotel, renowned for its linear architecture, unusual antique furnishings, and scripted ceiling borders, transported us back to the 1920s when Perry was a bustling railroad town. After an informative introduction in the ballroom area, amidst railroad memorabilia, we were free to wander through the building.

Our tour ended on the lower level of the hotel in the bowling alley. Here, a tour guide joined us again. She told us of the time capsule the town's second graders had placed here in celebration of the hotel's restoration. In the capsule, the children had put hand-written notes and contemporary items from stores. On the outside of their time capsule, they'd left explicit instructions that it not be opened for 100 years.

With our tour ended, we moseyed back to our cars. My friend enthusiastically suggested, "Wouldn't it be fun if we made a time capsule together, one like the second graders constructed!"

Not quite as enthusiastic, I asked, "What difference will it make to those who come after us by 100 years whether they have an idea of how we lived at the end of the 20th century?"

To which my friend replied, "It might not make a difference to them, but I think it will make a huge difference to us."

I gave her a puzzled look.

She explained how time capsules make us aware of how short our lives really are. They help us assess what's really important. And they show generations hence the role Christ played in our lives. But I still wasn't convinced. I didn't know whether I wanted to expend the time and energy this project would demand.

Several months later, on a morning when I wasn't thinking about time capsules or the conversation my friend and I had about them, I took out my devotional book. Turning to the day's Bible verse, I read, "As for me and my household, we will serve the LORD" (Joshua 24:15). It dawned on me: *If Joshua's words had not been recorded as a living expression of what he believed, I'd never have known what he and his family considered important in their lives.*

In that moment, I realized how essential it was that I too leave an expression of my faith, a quiet declaration that would tell generations after me the significance Christ has in my life. Perhaps I could encourage someone in their faith walk.

I began compiling the list of effects I wanted to leave in my time capsule—possessions, writings—and called my friend. "Still interested in making that time capsule together?"

Prayer

O Lord God, show me how—through time capsules, oral history, or written words—to leave behind expressions of my faith so others will know of Your power and presence in my life. Like Joshua, let me serve You and Your kingdom here on earth. In Jesus' saving name I pray. Amen.

Journal Jottings

Write how you will let others who come after you know how important God is to you.

Snap

FINDING THE POSITIVE

*Give thanks in all circumstances, for this
is God's will for you in Christ Jesus.*
1 Thessalonians 5:18

"Are we still having lunch together on Friday?" my friend phoned me the Wednesday before.

"Sure planning on it," I said. We had made plans to meet at our favorite luncheon spot at 1:00.

"Do you think you'll make it by then?" she asked. She knew I was squeezing in a doctor's appointment in another city 30 minutes away before meeting her.

"Sure do," I said without a qualm. If anything should come up, she wanted me to call her. I assured her I would, but not to worry. I wasn't expecting anything.

Friday dawned sunny with a light, crisp breeze. I felt invigorated. I finished my chores by 7:30 a.m. Then realizing I hadn't heard her alarm go off, I began moving in the direction of my daughter's bedroom. Before I'd reached her room, I heard a snap!

I knew by the wobbly feeling that I was in trouble. My brace had broken. Hobbling to the kitchen, I called my husband, relaying what had happened. Within minutes, he was home to assess the situation. After scrutinizing my brace, he spoke straightforwardly.

"You have a broken brace strap that needs to be fixed. As much as you'd like to keep your plans for the day with your friend, I'm afraid that is out of the question."

As I faced this change in plans, I couldn't help but recall the words I'd read earlier that morning from 1 Thessalonians 5:18, "Give thanks in all circumstances."

Picking up the phone to call my friend with the disheartening news, I asked the Lord, "How do You expect me to be thankful for this?"

After hearing the unfavorable news, my friend calmly said, "I'm thankful it wasn't something worse." It was clear to me she knew how to pull the positive, rather than the negative, out of disheartening situations.

After hanging up, taking my friend's cue, I began extracting from my present situation what I had to be thankful for. I was thankful the orthotist could fix my brace this day on such a quick notice. I was grateful my mom was willing to drop everything she'd planned to go with me to the brace shop. Finally, I was appreciative I didn't have to make another trip to the city, since I'd already planned to be there for another appointment.

From this simple exercise, I gained a new appreciation for Paul's words to the people of Thessalonica. When God empowered me to focus on the blessings of my unfortunate situation and not the disappointments, the situation didn't change—but my outlook did.

I started looking at other areas in my life that, at first glance, looked like disappointments—like my daughter not having a date for her junior prom and my sister not landing the university position closer to home.

Maybe, even in these less than desirable situations, the same can be true, I reminded myself. *Perhaps if I draw out what I can appreciate rather than what I might regret, though the situations won't change, my perspective will.*

In my daughter's situation, I was grateful she didn't succumb to peer pressure, willing to go out with anyone just to have a date for the prom. I was also thankful for the group of young women she did go to the prom with.

In my sister's circumstance, I was thankful for the good interviewing experience she was getting, the kind that would benefit her down the road. I was also grateful for the fulfilling job she was enjoying, only two-and-a-half hours from where we lived.

As God helps me see the donut rather than the hole, focus on the positive instead of the negative, think of the blessing not the disappointment, it truly will make a difference in how much I enjoy life. What a blessing that my brace snapped!

Prayer

Help me, Lord God, to find in each situation in life—especially the disheartening ones—all I can be thankful for rather than what I could regret. When things go wrong, remind me to trust You for all my needs. Strengthen me through Your Holy Spirit so I can be a witness to You in good times and in bad times. I pray in Jesus' name. Amen.

Journal Jottings

Identify an area in your life that makes you think of what is wrong instead of what is right. Write a prayer asking God to help you find the positive in it.

C'mon, Stay and Play
TAKING TIME TO HAVE FUN

There is a time for everything ...
a time to laugh. Ecclesiastes 3:1, 4

Following a mouth-watering Thanksgiving feast at my brother and sister-in-law's home, the men played armchair football in the living room and the women gathered around the kitchen table to talk. About mid-afternoon, as the conversation lulled, we heard loud knocking on the back door. In bolted my sister-in-law's niece with her 5-year-old son.

From the minute they dashed through the door, I noticed how spirited they were. The little guy raced around the table to give each of us a preschooler's bear hug, and his mother greeted us with a cheerful hello.

As the afternoon wore on, this single mother explained the reason for her joyful spirit. She admitted she'd had a difficult time growing up. Hoping for a fresh start, she had moved with her son a few months ago from her childhood home to Colorado. She had been working in a temporary job, but when they returned home from their Thanksgiving visit, she had a permanent job waiting for her. It was her first "real" job, one that held promise and potential for her.

After an early evening snack of turkey leftovers, I mentioned to my husband and daughter that we should go. My husband and I both had work to do. Since she'd driven another car, our daughter asked to stay longer. My sister-in-law's niece pleaded, "C'mon, please stay and play a game with us. You can work another time. We don't see each other that often."

I merely smiled. But when she fixed her eyes on me a second time, I sensed I should stay and be a part of the fun.

Yet because of our hectic holiday schedule and my writing deadlines, I decided to go home.

As I climbed into the car, my husband detected my regret. "I'm probably making the wrong choice," I admitted. "Oh, well, there will be plenty of other times." But all I could think of that evening, as my husband finished his chores and I stared blankly at my computer, was the fun I was missing.

A couple of hours later, our daughter returned, all wound up. "Oh, Mom. You should have been there. I've never laughed so much playing 'Gestures'."

This single mother and her son returned to Denver where she started her new job. A month later, while traveling to meet her parents on Christmas Eve, both mother and son were in a car accident that took their lives. I wish I hadn't missed that night's laughter.

Prayer

Despite life's endless demands, Lord God, remind me to take time to play and have fun, especially when loved ones implore me, lest I regret the gaiety and laughter I missed. Just as I need time to work, help me remember that I need time to laugh as well. Make me mindful of how short life on this earth really is. Help me use all of my days to Your glory. In Jesus' name I pray. Amen.

Journal Jottings

Tell of a time when you regretted not having taken the time to have fun and share a laugh or two. Why do you regret it?

Second Thoughts

MY CONFIDENCE LEVEL

Search me, O God, and know my heart;
test me and know my anxious thoughts.
Psalm 139:23

Late one spring morning, as I sat in my pastoral counselor's office, he said, "I suspect you could be a lot less critical of yourself and a lot less anxious if you didn't spend so much time second-guessing your decisions."

Although I gave him a "you-don't-know-what-you're-talking-about" look, he offered a suggestion. For the next couple of weeks, I was to keep track of the number of times I second-guessed myself. I was convinced the assignment would be a cinch, since I believed that I was confident in my decisions.

While at the beauty salon that afternoon, I decided, on the spur of the moment, to change my hairstyle. When I got home, my husband complimented my "new 'do."

Rather than graciously accepting his compliment, I blurted out, "I probably should have kept it the way I had it before. I'm sure I won't be able to fix it as cute as my stylist did." *Oops, I second-guessed myself. Oh, well, everyone's entitled to at least one blunder.*

That same evening, when my daughter returned home, I told her about the dress I'd bought for her. It was hanging in the foyer closet in the store's signature bag.

As she pulled up the bag to examine the dress, I apologized for probably not picking out the right one. If she preferred, I said, I could exchange it for another.

My daughter replied, "Mom, you haven't even given me a chance to try on this one. I'm sure it will look great. Don't backtrack on your decisions so much."

In just a few hours, I'd already questioned my decisions twice. *Not a very good record for an assignment that was supposed to be a cinch,* I thought. Maybe my counselor was on to something after all.

I was determined not to let the pattern keep happening. The next day, I received yet another test.

After giving our Sunday school class a devotion I'd written, my husband and I gave the students a chance to read it before we discussed its theme. When one of our students complimented my writing, instead of offering up my usual, "I probably should have explained the ending better," I caught myself. "I'm glad it spoke to you," I warmly responded.

While I might still struggle with second-guessing my own choices, I know with all confidence that I need never second-guess God's love for me. He sees beyond my weaknesses, and makes Himself real to me through Word and Sacrament. His hope has become my hope.

Prayer

Heavenly Father, give me confidence in my decisions rather than being critical and second-guessing choices I've made. Send Your Holy Spirit to strengthen my faith in You so I will have a less anxious heart, the kind You desire. Help me, Lord, find peace in the security of Your promise of salvation. In Your Son's name I pray. Amen.

Journal Jottings

What choices have you recently made where you've second-guessed yourself? How did your choices result?

Toppling Eggs

WHEN WE TUMBLE

I have become like broken pottery.
Psalm 31:12

That particular morning, I felt like "Humpty Dumpty," the egg in the children's nursery rhyme that tumbled off the wall and broke into so many pieces no one could put it back together. Let me explain.

About 12 months before, I had my right full-length leg brace replaced. This came as no surprise, since the one I'd been wearing for 15 years had worn out. When I had gotten the mechanical wrinkles worked out of my new brace, however, my orthotist suggested I brace the other leg too because of the post-polio weakness I was experiencing.

As if this wasn't enough tumbling off the wall, once I was able to maneuver both braces successfully, I discovered that none of my shoes fit over my new braces. I needed shoes a whole width wider. But there wasn't a store or catalog I knew of that carried the wider width.

This is why I felt like Humpty Dumpty that morning. Despite what my reassuring husband and well-meaning orthotist did to "put me back together," their efforts never seemed to be enough. With every move I made, another little piece of my life seemed to topple.

Like the psalmist, I felt like I had "become like broken pottery" (Psalm 31:12). *Would I ever be intact again?* I wondered.

Mine wasn't the only life tumbling. Many of my friends were feeling like cracked, toppled eggs themselves. One friend wrote asking for guidance to keep her marriage from falling apart. Another sought advice on handling concerns about her aging parents. Still another friend wanted me to suggest ways she could comfort and care for a dying friend.

It was while I was thinking of these problems that I thought of the nursery rhyme. I repeated its lilting words: "Humpty Dumpty sat on a wall, Humpty Dumpty had a great fall. All the king's horses and all the king's men, couldn't put Humpty together again."

Although my heart ached for my friends, nothing I could do could fully satisfy or give them the answers they were seeking. Neither could I receive an adequate resolution for the problems confronting me. For the rest of the week, I tried to ignore these problems while I went on with each day's concerns.

The Lord knew what I needed to hear. The following Sunday in church, near the end of the sermon, my pastor pulled out a tattered volume of Mother Goose from which his mother had read to him when he was a child. He read "Humpty Dumpty" aloud. He ended his sermon with a quote from a colleague who speculated on how this rhyme might have been finished. "If 'all the king's horses and all the king's men couldn't put Humpty together again,' then why didn't they do the obvious—call upon the King?"

The message hit home. Life brings problems, and sometimes there is little I can do to keep my life or the lives of my friends from toppling over. Nor can I—on my own— put my life back together.

Strengthened by my faith in Christ, however, I can avoid falling to pieces. I can rely on God's Word and grace through His sacraments to restore me to wholeness once again. I can grasp the thread of hope God extends and use it to bind me to His gift of life in my Savior.

As I wobbled out of church that morning, with my husband and daughter two steps ahead of me, I resolved to put my problems squarely in God's hands. I would call upon the King.

Prayer

Heavenly Father, I am like Humpty Dumpty, a broken egg. When life's problems threaten to make me topple over, I get anxious because there is little I can do on my own to put the pieces back together. Help me to do the obvious—to call on You for help. You alone have the power to repair my broken life. Make me ever mindful of the stability You offer through Jesus' life-giving sacrifice for me. In His name I pray. Amen.

Journal Jottings

Make a list of the people you know who are toppling over from the weight of life's problems. Pray for them by name.

Alone with Mom in I. C. U.

BEING LEFT MOTHERLESS

*For to me, to live is Christ and to die is
gain ... I am torn between the two:
I desire to depart and be with Christ,
which is better by far; but it is more
necessary for you that I remain in the
body. Philippians 1:21, 23*

Mom, I screamed inside. *You can't do this to me. You
can't leave me motherless.*

I was alone with my mother in the intensive care unit
following her open-heart surgery. As I studied her lifeless-
looking body, there were so many questions I wanted to
ask her.

Did she know how much I loved her? Had I thanked her
enough for all the sacrifices she'd made for me through the
years, or did she think they had gone unnoticed?

I noticed the crisp white sheet covering her. She
appeared so helplessly vulnerable as the ventilator forced
her to breathe. *Lord, how will my life go on without her?
Can it ever be the same?*

As I looked at the charts, tubes, and ghastly complex
machines that monitored her vital signs, her heartbeat was
the only recognizable sign of life I could detect. Her eye-
lids were tightly closed. They had been all day. Clearly, she
couldn't communicate with me nor I with her. Her life, I
sensed, was somehow between the two kingdoms my pastor had often talked about.

My hands felt cold and clammy, yet my back was soaked with perspiration. Emotionally spent, I kept praying. How hard it was for me to accept that my mother's life might be at an end.

Then, in that moment amid the tubes and monitors, I remembered that Jesus promises to be with me always. I felt His presence and His reassurance that no matter what my mother's outcome, I'd be all right. The faith the Holy Spirit had given in her in Baptism dwelt in me also.

I recalled how Paul had spoken similar words to Timothy to reassure him. "To Timothy, my beloved child ... I am reminded of your sincere faith, a faith that lived first in your grandmother Lois and your mother Eunice and now, I am sure, lives in you" (2 Timothy 1:2, 5 NRSV).

As Christ reassured me with these words from Scripture, He gave me the strength to accept whatever my Heavenly Father had in mind for my mother. I'd been tenaciously holding on to my past. In that moment, Christ helped me give up my childhood. I'd been frightened about losing my mother. He eased that too. Christ had revealed Himself through Scripture, and through the power of the Holy Spirit He became real to me in a deeper way—heart, soul, and spirit—than I'd ever thought possible.

I believe my mother survived because of Christ's infinite grace to me. Because of this experience, the love between us has grown even deeper. No longer do I see our love as a dependent one but as a shared one—sustained through the love of Christ Himself. I know that when my mother leaves this earthly home, she will go to her heavenly home which Christ has prepared for her.

Until that time, I'm letting go of the past, embracing the present, and thanking Him for each additional day that my mother and I share together.

Prayer

Dearest Savior, reassure me that when my loved ones die, You will provide comfort, sustenance, and healing. Help me to live my life as a witness to my faith in Your unfailing love. And eventually, bring me to my home in heaven where there will be no more partings. In Your saving name I pray. Amen.

Journal Jottings

Write your thoughts about losing a parent, friend, or someone else especially close to you.

Ladies' Church Luncheon

"For My thoughts are not your thoughts,
neither are your ways My ways,"
declares the LORD. Isaiah 55:8

Unlike all the other chilly, damp days during our week-long stay with my parents in Florida, the weather forecast promised that the next day would be sunny and warm. *A perfect day to walk the beach and lay out by the pool,* I thought as I pulled out my swimsuit and suntan lotion.

Just then, Mom stepped into our bedroom and invited me to her ladies' church luncheon (held annually for the snowbirds who would be returning north).

The look on my face gave me away. She quickly added, "Oh, don't let me keep you from what you've already planned to do."

That night, I couldn't stop thinking about Mom's invitation. I knew if I didn't go with her, I'd feel guilty. If I went, though, I'd regret not soaking up the rays on the last day of my visit. I prayed, "Lord, going with Mom to her ladies' church group and luncheon isn't how I intended to spend my final day of vacation. Still, I don't want to disappoint her because she's been so good to us while we've been here." I felt myself drifting off to sleep while still asking Him for direction.

I awoke with the sun cutting blades of light through the blinds. Dad peeked his head in wondering what I'd decided to do about Mom's offer. Before I could answer, he said, "This group of ladies down here has done a lot for your mother. I'm so happy she's gotten to know them as her friends." With that comment, although I still preferred spending the day on the beach, I sensed Christ was nudging me elsewhere.

Mom was so proud introducing me to her friends that day, each lady unique, bonded together by their love for Christ and one another. After lunch, we took Eleanor, a close friend of my mother's, home. As she was getting out of the car, she asked if we would have some iced tea and cookies with her.

Before we knew it, we'd chatted the whole afternoon away. Even then, she wouldn't let us go without showing us her new computer and writing her e-mail address for me. I was inspired by this remarkable 80-year-old Christian woman.

That night, back in the condo, I thought about how memorable the day had been and how glad I was that I had accepted Mom's invitation. I would take from this day a wonderful memory and the thread that ties my mom and myself together. And God knew I couldn't have suntanned anyway. Sand squalls had ruled the beach all day.

Prayer

Lord Jesus, when I've planned to do something specific with my time, yet You nudge in another direction, help me to listen. Although it may not seem like it at the time, Your timing is perfect and Your nudge will always turn out to be the better option. Help me to follow You in all things. In Your name I pray. Amen.

Journal Jottings

Tell about a time when you had made plans, but you felt the Holy Spirit guiding you in another direction.

A Chunk of Dead Wood

LIFE STILL HOLDS PURPOSE

They will still bear fruit in old age.
Psalm 92:14

When our family of three moved to the farmhouse where the old cottonwood tree stood, my husband and I thought it'd be best to cut the aged tree down. "It's only a chunk of dead wood," I said.

"Don't make your decision too quickly," my dad said. He went on to explain. Years ago, when he wanted to saw this same cottonwood tree down, Dad's brother cautioned him to think twice. This particular tree, he said, was positioned in such a way that it would take a bolt of lightning in place of buildings or people. My dad continued, "that's why I've never wanted to cut this tree down."

Yielding to Dad's suggestion, we granted the cottonwood a reprieve. Shortly after that, an event occurred that made his words seem almost prophetic.

It happened on a Father's Day. Mom and I were in the kitchen finishing the dinner dishes, and my husband and father were channel surfing in the living room to catch the latest storm reports. With a crack of thunder so intense the dishes rattled, lightning buried itself into our cottonwood. The energy of the bolt blew bark off the tree, shattering our living room window. For a moment, we were numb. Regaining our senses, we rushed outside to assess the damage and discovered a deep, ugly gash from crown to trunk, one that would take the tree several seasons to recover from. The cottonwood had taken the hit, saving the next highest object—our house—from considerable damage.

I looked at the tree as the last rays of daylight filtered through its damaged branches with one thought. I had believed the old, old tree was useless, "a chunk of dead wood." It wasn't. I was reminded of another old, old "tree"—Morrie.

A professor from Brandeis University, Massachusetts, Morrie contracted Lou Gehrig's disease (ALS) at the age of 78. In his last month, bedridden and in pain, he taught what could be called his greatest lesson.

He dictated this final lesson to a former student, Mitch Albom. On 14 consecutive Tuesdays, Mitch recorded this "one final lesson on how to live." The book which resulted was titled *Tuesdays with Morrie*. It became a best-selling book and a movie.

Both the old cottonwood and the old professor could have been thought of as just "a chunk of dead wood." But after a long, useful life, both were examples of Psalm 92:14. "They will still bear fruit in old age, they will stay fresh and green" (Psalm 92:14).

Prayer

Lord God, thank You for the blessing of a long, useful life. But even when I'm worn and spent, help me never to regard myself as merely "dead wood." Give me hope that I may always bear fruit for You. Remind me, that while I have breath, I am a valued part of Your kingdom on earth and can always live as a witness to the victory over death we all have in Christ Jesus. In Jesus' name I pray. Amen.

Journal Jottings

Describe someone you know who is still bearing fruit for God in their old age.

Choir Is Coming

CHALLENGING THE IMPOSSIBLE

Jesus replied, "What is impossible with
men is possible with God." Luke 18:27

When I picked up the phone that evening, it was my daughter's youth sponsor from church. "Our youth group is responsible for housing the college concert choir the night they sing in our church. Can I count on you for beds?"

I knew my daughter would enjoy having a couple of college girls stay with us, especially since she was interested in music. With my limited strength, however, a commitment like this seemed impossible. "I really would like to help, but I just don't have enough strength."

She understood and said she would find someone else. My daughter, clearly disheartened, left the room quietly.

The next Sunday in church, another sponsor approached me in front of my daughter asking if I'd reconsider housing a couple of choir members. Although I felt guilty declining a second time, I believed a task like this was out of the question for me. I gave a less persuasive excuse than before. We didn't have room.

Yet a third time, a few nights later, when another advisor brought our daughter home from basketball practice, she begged me to rethink my decision and put up two choir kids. Desiring to, and by now feeling terribly guilty, I almost said yes. That is, until I imagined what an unworkable scenario I'd be getting myself into. I gave the flimsiest reason of all. It would interfere too much with my writing.

A year later, our church bulletin announced another college choir coming. Again the youth group sponsors were recruiting bed and breakfast for the choir. This time, before I could raise any excuses for not hosting two of the members, my daughter said, "Mom, instead of shrugging this experience off again, why don't you try and change your perspective? Why don't you see it as 'doable'? After all, you've always told me what is impossible with us is possible—doable—with God" (Luke 18:27).

I listened with chagrin and skepticism and relented. We would take in two of the girls. With those words out of my mouth, all I could do now was rely on God's power to make this experience doable.

We had no extra beds, so we simply pulled out the "sleeper" love seat and made use of the couch. We stayed up late visiting with the guests we hosted, but God gave me the strength to wake up early the next morning and fix our guests a stick-to-your-ribs breakfast. My writing time was even enhanced because I received a couple of new ideas. And my daughter gave me a new word to add to my vocabulary—"doable."

Prayer

Lord God, when a job I'm asked to do appears impossible, help me to alter my perspective. Guide me to rely on Your power so I see my tasks as doable. Remind me to open my heart and home to Your servants and to enjoy the fellowship we share in You. In Jesus' name I pray. Amen.

Journal Jottings

Think about a task that you're avoiding. Tell how, with God's help, you can make it "doable."

Aboard the Mooney

TRUSTING CHRIST AS MY PILOT

Then I saw a new heaven. ...
Revelation 21:1

My brother-in-law's plane is as important to him as my writing is to me. That's why I decided to accept Tim's offer to fly with him in his plane—although it put me into a cold sweat.

My heart was pounding as he helped me awkwardly climb the wing step into his Mooney, a single prop, high performance airplane. I crawled into the cramped cockpit and immediately fastened my seat belt. My husband and daughter squeezed into the cabin with me. After securing the door, Tim did a careful instrument check, making certain we were ready for take-off. After receiving clearance from the tower, we were sky bound, climbing to an altitude of 3,000 feet.

Once airborne, Tim adjusted the prop, the pitch, and the engine rpms. We were now set to cruise. Reaching back, gently touching my knees, he said, "Trust me. I will bring you home safely." He told me to sit back, enjoy the ride, and leave the piloting to him.

Despite his good intentions, there was some turbulence in the sky that day that couldn't be avoided. In a way, it was just like the unavoidable turbulence in my life right then. My dad was scheduled for an MRI to help doctors determine why he had suffered dramatic hearing loss in one ear. Some family members were coping with how to raise a baby boy born with Down's Syndrome. I was struggling to wear a new full-length brace on what had been my good leg.

Surprisingly enough, despite this turbulence, both in the sky and in my life, I relaxed when Tim said, "Trust me. I will bring you home safely." Why? I heard Christ speaking these exact words at precisely the same moment in my heart. I was reasonably sure, despite the pockets of turbulence jarring our Mooney that day, that Tim, our pilot, would land us safely home. He did.

More important, after that day, I was even more sure of my faith in Christ to steer me through all of life's turbulent journey. As my Pilot, His intentions to bring me safely home were so strong He was willing to become human and die on a cross to get me there.

All I need to do now is to sit back, relax, and enjoy the ride, leaving the piloting to Him.

Prayer

Thank You for promising me, Lord Jesus, to pilot me safely through the turbulence of this life to my eternal home in heaven. By dying on the cross, resurrecting, and ascending home Yourself, You already affirmed You will do this. Help me enjoy the ride home with You, leaving the piloting to You. In Your name I pray. Amen.

Journal Jottings

Note an area in your life where you need to leave the piloting to Christ. Give this area to Him in prayer.

My Daughter's First Date
COMING UP SHORT

"Lift up your heads." Luke 21:28

As I stood in the living room that night, aware how quickly our daughter had grown up, I felt a sense of bitter sweetness. I was joyful our daughter had become the lovely debutante I saw awaiting her first date, yet sad, knowing the innocent, carefree days of her childhood had been whisked away.

Watching our daughter depart hand-in-hand with her date for the homecoming dance, attired in her purple suede suit, reminded me of another time she'd left. Dressed in a purple play suit, bound for kindergarten, she tightly clutched her daddy's strong arm as he drove her down our long lane to meet the school bus. I had the same questions now as then. *Had I done everything I could to prepare her for this next phase of life? Had I been the perfect parent I wanted to be?*

I returned to my writing. Then I remembered—until I found the exact words to "Humpty Dumpty," I couldn't finish what I was writing.

After finding the poem, instantly, a cloudburst of regrets started pouring over me. I reminisced about the many times I should have read this poem and others like it to my daughter. Due to my fatigue by the end of the day, I hadn't. *If only I'd found that extra surge of strength,* I lamented.

A few minutes later, as I picked up the ringing phone, regret grabbed me again. *If I'd only encouraged my daughter while she was younger to invite more friends over, perhaps as a teen she'd have more people calling her.*

Later, I glanced at the calendar of school events posted on the refrigerator door. *I wish I'd prioritized my writing schedule more to accommodate her school activities.*

It was strikingly clear to me. I'd come up way short of being the perfect parent I'd desired to be. I hadn't lived up to the expectations I'd set for myself. *So how can I live with this reality?* I wondered.

A few days later, while sitting in the pastoral counselor's office recounting my parenting regrets, my counselor stopped me. "Now tell me what you did well as a parent." That list was much harder for me to frame.

First, I recalled how I'd usually been home when my daughter came from school. That allowed me the opportunity to listen to the ups and downs of her day while they were fresh in her mind.

Second, I recollected by being my daughter's close friend, I'd shown her what true friendship was all about. I hoped this example would guide her in years to come as she chose her life-long friends.

The counselor added, "Whether or not you are aware of it, your daughter has been watching you write all of these years. From observing you, she's learned such things as perseverance, determination, and goal setting." Then he asked if this exercise had taught me anything.

"I guess I didn't miss the mark in parenting as much as I thought I had," I offered.

He told me to lift up my head. I was being much too hard on myself. I'd been a good parent, not a perfect one, just like he had been.

The reality is that none of us, despite our best intentions, can hit the mark of perfect parenting. Our heavenly Father is the only perfect parent, loving all His children to the point that He sacrificed His own Son to pay for the sins of the world.

As I left his office that day, I felt like a weight had been lifted. I hadn't done everything right as a parent. Neither had I done it all wrong. No, I hadn't been a perfect parent, but, assuredly, God had helped me be a good one.

Prayer

O Lord God, thank You for being a perfect Father, for sending Your Son to give His life for my sins. Help me to serve You by giving my best to my child. Strengthen my faith so I can put all my trust in You to guide me as I parent her. Having done that, may I confidently raise my head, leaving the rest of her growing up to You. In Your Son's name I pray. Amen.

Journal Jottings

When you come up short of your aspirations, take your journal out and write: ***I've tried, but I'm not perfect.*** Then write a prayer thanking God for sending His perfect Son for you.

Allyson's Sandals
LOOKING OUTSIDE

"Man looks at the outward appearance,
but the LORD looks at the heart."
1 Samuel 16:7

Sitting with our high school Sunday school class, my husband and I, as facilitators, tossed out a question. "Have you ever misjudged a person because of their appearance?" I was a little smug as they started relating their stories. This had never been a problem for me. Or was I wrong? I started reviewing my memories.

One of those memories had taken place at my parent's condo in Florida where my husband, daughter, daughter's friend Allyson, and I were vacationing.

After walking along the beach one morning, my husband and I returned to the condo. As we opened the door we saw Allyson looking frantically for something. When we inquired if anything was wrong, we were told that Allyson's favorite sandals were missing. It wasn't long before each of us was combing through every nook and cranny in the condo, looking for the sandals.

When we all came up with nothing but a few dust balls, Allyson began retracing her steps, thinking of the places she might have left them. Finally she said, "I think I left them down by the pool."

As she breezed out the door to go down to the pool, my father stopped her. "With the turnover there's been in this place recently and with this younger generation on spring break, running around in their sparse bikinis and wild swimming trunks, if your sandals were down by the pool, they probably aren't there anymore." I heartily agreed.

A few minutes later, Allyson came back beaming. She'd found her sandals by the pool beneath a lounge chair. My father and I were proven wrong about the young people in the area.

Give me a break, I told myself. That's only one time I've misjudged people by their appearance alone.

While the high schoolers went on recounting their own stories, another memory surfaced. This one occurred in the airport only a few days after the episode with Allyson's sandals.

After retrieving our suitcases at the baggage claim, my husband offered to bring the car around while we waited with our luggage. I started visiting with a lady sitting beside me. She and her husband had just retired from work in the Philippines. She told me they were now moving to a house close to their son and daughter. As we talked, her son and daughter approached.

Studying this 30-something son with his long ponytail and dangling earrings, sloppy blue jeans and over-sized denim shirt, I drew one conclusion. "Bet, unlike his hard-working dad, he hasn't lifted a finger his entire life."

Just then, my husband pulled up with the car. Our daughter carried out our luggage. Before she could return for me, this long-haired, what appeared to me, ill-kept man gently asked if he could push my wheelchair to the car. Taken aback by his kindness, I nodded yes.

Oops. Again my opinion was formed by looking at a person's appearance—and in less than a week's time.

I had learned through the prophet Samuel that God does not judge people by their outward appearance but assesses them by looking at their hearts (1 Samuel 16:7). I knew I hadn't followed His example. Twice on vacation alone I'd judged people entirely by how they looked.

Our Savior was different from the religious leaders of His day, and He was judged by what they saw in Him: a threat to their status and their way of life. Had His judges been able to see Jesus' heart, they would have recognized Him as the Messiah, the fulfillment of God's promise of salvation.

Guess I'd better confess to our young adults how this problem has crept up on me too, I thought. As the youth finished telling of their experiences, I cleared my throat. "More than I'd like to admit ..." I began.

Prayer

Forgive me, dear heavenly Father, for the times I've formed the wrong opinion of people because I've judged them by their appearance and not by their hearts. Open my heart to others so I can rejoice in the differences You create in us. And show me how to share the peace and joy that comes from Your grace bestowed upon me. In Jesus' name I pray. Amen.

Journal Jottings

Recount a blunder in judging by appearance only.

Computer Salesman

*Let us not love with words or tongue but
with actions and in truth. 1 John 3:18*

Do actions speak louder than words? The least likely place for me to discover the answer was in an upscale suburban computer store. Yet that is how it happened.

Late one frigid Saturday afternoon in January, my husband, teenage daughter, and I went to such a store. Countless computers making chirping sounds surrounded us. Feeling intimidated, I whispered, "I suppose we'd better find someone who can help us." No sooner had I said this than a salesperson approached, asking if he could assist us.

After demonstrating the computer he felt would best fit our needs, he commented, "I'm low on this model. We've been offering a special price on it for several weeks. I'll give you some time to decide what you want to do. Meanwhile, I'll check the inventory to make sure one is even available in our store."

After he left, another salesperson reached right in front of us, grabbed a component from the system we'd been looking at, and sold it to another customer. Our salesperson, having seen this as he returned, went back to check the inventory again. Unfortunately this one was the last complete model in the store. He apologized profusely. All he could do was issue us a rain check and try to locate one for us in other stores.

Although it would be easy to get angry or upset, I thought, *if I call myself a Christian, I should act like one.*

We thanked him for his time and patience. We'd wait to see if he could find a model like this somewhere else.

A few weeks later, our salesperson called, telling us the computer we'd earmarked was in. We told him we'd be there Friday to pick it up. Friday was his day off, he said, but he would be there anyway.

He greeted us as we entered the store. After making small talk, he sat down with us, explaining the warranty package. Upon signing the sales agreement, he asked us about our livelihood. My husband explained briefly about our farming operation, then told him I managed the book-keeping. "But her passion is Christian devotional writing," he added.

"I thought you might be Christians by the way you acted," he said. I looked at him quizzically. "When you couldn't get the computer you wanted the first day, when it was sold right from under you, you didn't get angry or upset. That usually doesn't happen."

"I'm a Christian too," he continued. "Here, though, I have to witness in more subtle ways."

I picked up the conversation. "Is one of those ways working on your day off to take care of customers like us?" I asked. Then I added, "Maybe we speak more about our faith by how we act than by what we say."

"You mean, actions speak louder than words?" he asked.

I nodded. It was a lesson learned unexpectedly.

Prayer

Gracious God, thank You for what You have done for me through the death and resurrection of Jesus Christ. Remind me that my actions speak of who I am and Whose I am far more often than my words do. And never let me forget that through Christ I can forgive others, because You first forgave me. In Christ's name. Amen.

Journal Jottings

Explain a time in your life when your actions spoke louder than your words.

Why?

WHEN A YOUNG PERSON DIES

"In my Father's house are many rooms;
if it were not so, I would have told you.
I am going there to prepare a place
for you." John 14:2

When Mary and Joseph arrived at the Jerusalem temple, according to Jewish tradition, to present their child to the Lord, death was probably the farthest thing from their minds. That is until Simeon, taking baby Jesus in his arms, looked at Mary and prophesied, "A sword will pierce your own soul too" (Luke 2:35).

As Mary left the temple that day, she must have had many questions. What did this prophecy mean? What would her baby boy face? What would happen to pierce her soul?

As with Mary, I'm sure death was about the farthest word from my friend's mind that Christmas Eve when she and her husband drove to meet their daughter and grandson to celebrate Christmas. They were scheduled to rendezvous later that evening at a comfortable hotel midway between their respective homes.

When several hours passed with daughter and grandson not arriving, they became distraught with fear. After numerous calls to the police, they discovered their daughter had lost her life in a car accident, just minutes from the hotel. Their grandson lay in a nearby hospital in critical condition, given little hope of survival.

As this mother and father listened to this painful news, this woman's broken, anguished heart, I imagine, cried out like Mary's when she watched her Son give up His life for the sins of the world. "Why did this happen? Why did death intrude on my happiness and hush my expectations?" I'm sure she, like Mary, knew life never again would be the same.

Why did death invade Mary's life? Why does it invade ours?

It was through Christ's death that our eternal life was born. "For God so loved the world that He gave His one and only Son, that whoever believes in Him shall not perish but have eternal life" (John 3:16). St. Francis of Assissi penned this truth so beautifully years ago when he wrote, "It is in dying that we are born to eternal life."

Born to eternal life through Baptism, we are assured of a life far greater than we know here. For Christ Himself promised, just before He left this earthly dwelling, "to go to His Father's house to prepare a place for us" (John 14:2, paraphrased).

Sad though my friend be, she knows, and I know, her daughter and grandson are celebrating Christmas with another Mother and Son, Mary and Jesus.

Prayer

Thank You, heavenly Father, for the assurance of eternal life, born through Christ's own death on the cross. Hallelujah! In Christ's name. Amen.

Journal Jottings

Tell about a loved one whose passing meant they were born to something greater.

Two Sand Dollars

Two are better than one ... a cord of
three strands is not quickly broken.
Ecclesiastes 4:9a, 12b

Walking along the beach in Florida, I saw two sand dollars wash ashore, encrusted upon one another. Their size and worn edges indicated age. They hadn't always been together. At one time, they'd floated their separate paths. *What an apt symbol for my relationship with my sister.*

Two sand dollars floating separately in the sea of life—at times all but colliding and damaging the other. This describes the relationship I had with my sister in our growing-up years. We both strove to be on top, to be better than the other. This was often achieved by being opposites.

My sister, six years younger, enjoyed being outdoors, surrounded by animals, the "Pied Piper," our family would call her. I preferred being inside in my reading nook, surrounded with my books. Her teenage pursuits were large slumber parties and many girlfriends. I opted for having my one close girlfriend stay overnight with me. I'd select a long, frilly dress. She'd choose a short, no-frills, practical one. In almost every area of our life, we worked hard at distinguishing ourselves from the other.

When I left for college, much to my amazement, I missed my other sand dollar. She likewise missed me. When I'd return home over breaks, for awhile our two sand dollars were quite compatible. After a few days, when familiarity set in, we'd again collide.

Two sand dollars drifting in the sea of life—would we ever have the same mind-set?

Near the end of my second year of teaching, a boyfriend I'd developed a serious relationship with broke up with me. To ease my trauma, my sister drove four hours to stay with me the day I was jilted. When she left, I remember thinking, *Maybe, instead of looking out only for our own ambitions, striving to continuously out-do each other, our lives someday will merge.* Sadly, this was not meant to be, not yet anyway.

Even in our teaching careers, our moss-covered shells began scarring each other. Though no hurt was intended, it was all I could do to keep my jealousy from bubbling over. I started my teaching career in a parochial school. She began hers in a public one. I achieved an M.A. in Education. She received a Ph.D. in the same field. Due to my limited strength, I had to give up my career to start my family. She continued her career while raising her family.

Two sand dollars drifting in the sea of life—would we ever come together? Many years passed.

While in Florida for my 40th birthday, my sister spear-headed my birthday extravaganza. She suddenly turned and excused herself. We learned later that she'd had a miscarriage.

After all these years of watching my sister achieve more than I could hope for, all these years of continuously feeling like she had an edge over me, finally, I could help her. What's more, because of this incident, something else far more subtle happened.

When my sister returned from the hospital, it didn't matter what each of us had accomplished or which road we'd taken to get there. All that counted was that we were there for one another, easing the other's hurts, looking out for the other's interests, even participating in the other's dreams.

Our hearts and our thinking had, through God, been united. Like the waves ebb and flow, so would we. At one point, she'd be the leader; I the follower. At another, our roles would reverse. God would be woven through it all.

Although we drift in our separate worlds—she as a wife, mother, and university professor; I as a wife, mother, and writer—when we need each other, we're there for each other. *Two sand dollars—though two, at times we seem like we're floating, encrusted, as one.* Together we continue to discover anew the bond of sisterhood.

Prayer

Remind me, heavenly Father, that in relationships it doesn't matter who appears to have the edge. In Your eyes, none of this is important. All that counts is that we're there for one another at the foot of the cross, bound with the same purpose and vision. Thus, I will discover anew the joy You intended for such a relationship. In Christ's name I pray. Amen.

Journal Jottings

Write about the relationship you have with a sibling, friend, or relative and how that bond pulls you together when you need one another.

Undeserving

Jesus said, "It is not the healthy who
need a doctor, but the sick."
Matthew 9:12

"Since I haven't gotten to play in the last four varsity basketball games," our daughter called from school that morning, "the coach asked me to play in the junior varsity game tonight."

I detected a despondent tone in her voice.

"Will you and Dad be coming to watch me play?" she begged. We'd already gone to a number of games she didn't get to play in, and were behind in our work. I told her we'd talk about it over lunch and let her know when she called back.

At lunch, after discussing the situation in great detail, we came to the same conclusion. Had our daughter done the things her coach suggested during off season: practicing free throws, working on lay-ups, and taking up track, she'd probably be playing more varsity now. Since she hadn't, why should we drive 60 miles for a junior varsity game? If she'd tried harder, she'd be more than a "bench warmer" in the varsity games.

When our daughter called at noon, we told her why we wouldn't be coming. I could hear her spirit sink.

While folding laundry that afternoon, I began thinking of the Bible verse from Matthew that said something about the sick needing a doctor and not the healthy (Matthew 9:12). *Was Christ trying to tell me that people need us more when they're weak than when they're strong, regardless of how much they've tried?*

I thought of needy people I knew and their stories.

What if a family member had told her brother, when he was imprisoned for an alcohol-related offense and emotionally breakable, that he hadn't tried hard enough to overcome his addiction and didn't deserve her visit?

Or what if we, as employers, had told an employee, when he was debt-laden and emotionally spent, that we wouldn't advance his wages to pay for his wife's medicines because he hadn't worked hard enough to pull himself out of his financial slump? He wasn't worthy of such a favor.

Far worse, what if Christ had said to me He wasn't going to traipse all the way to earth on account of me? I wasn't worthy of His presence, much less of His dying for me, because I hadn't tried hard enough to be the person He wanted me to be.

In all three scenarios, this certainly wasn't the case. Our family member was there for her brother. We helped our employee. And Christ rescued me although I had done nothing to deserve His gift of salvation.

In that moment, I decided we'd be there for our daughter, regardless of whether she'd tried hard enough or was deserving of our presence.

When our daughter saw us in the bleachers that night as she was warming up on the court, she beamed. Her smile said, "I knew you'd come for me."

Prayer

Remind me, merciful God, it is when people are in their weaker moments that they need my encouragement the most. It doesn't matter whether they're deserving of help or whether they've tried hard enough to help themselves.

Keep me rooted in Your Word and make me ever aware You came for me, not because I was strong, but because I was "sick and in need of a doctor." In Your Son's compassionate name I pray. Amen.

Journal Jottings

Tell about a time when you rendered attention to a person who needed encouragement without thinking if they were worthy or whether they'd put forth enough effort.

Sand Sculpture

*So God created humankind in His
image. Genesis 1:27 NRSV*

While vacationing in Florida, my husband and I decided to take a stroll on the beach. The tide, on its way out, had deposited a bed of smooth, fine, white sand. *A perfect canvas for a sand artist,* I thought.

After having taken only a few steps, we came upon such a craftsman. We watched as the artist took sand and water, meticulously molding these ordinary elements into the shape of a human being. After forming the calves and thighs of his figure, he moved to its buttocks, then to the swell of its back, upward to its shoulders, arms, and neck, finally creating a head with flowing hair. Satisfied that he'd created his best, the sculptor carefully walked around his figure, touching it one last time. Picking up his pail of water and emptying it in the ocean, he left.

Later, relaxing on the patio of the condo, I watched as people passed by the sculpture. Some took time to gaze and study. A few barely noticed. Several others stood in awe as they revered the figure carved in the sand. After a while, some children traipsed by, stepped on the figure, and trampled it down. All that remained was its rough outline.

As I continued watching, to my astonishment, the artist returned. Seeing his devastated sculpture, he sat down with his hands cupped over his face. With the tide ready to come in again, I thought he had no reason to rebuild it. The waves would just wash away his masterpiece. Despite his disappointment, he must have loved his sculpture, for there by the ocean's edge, he squatted one more time. Salvaging, rebuilding, and resculpting, even more painstakingly than before, he restored the remains to its original state.

The message etched in the sand that day was simple yet profound. I am that sculpture. I have been destroyed and devastated by sin.

Although God could have chosen to leave me in this pitiful state, He didn't. Moved by compassion blended with grief, He squatted to salvage what was left of me, to recreate me, resculpt me. Entering my world in the form of Jesus, He reclaimed me as His own through Christ's death and resurrection. Through Christ, as a baptized, redeemed child of God, I am resculpted and renewed in His image.

Prayer

I thank You, O God, for resculpting me, restoring my fallen image, reclaiming me after I've sinned, through Your powerful yet painful act of redemption. In our precious Savior's name, who renews me through His body and blood, I pray. Amen.

Journal Jottings

Read the creation story in Genesis. Then read the story of the crucifixion and resurrection in any of the gospels, where they record how Christ resculpted and redeemed us. Record your thoughts.

Mother's Day Plans
OVERCOMING STUBBORNNESS

Honor your father and your mother.
Exodus 20:12

I couldn't wait any longer for my sister to call about her plans for Mother's Day, because the restaurants in our area would soon be booked. *I'll just include them,* I thought. I made a reservation for our entire family.

Two nights later, my sister called. With bubbling enthusiasm she chattered about a reservation she'd made for all of us at a restaurant located midway between our homes.

Why does my sister do this to me? Why does she think we should change our plans to accommodate hers? I silently fumed. Even if Mother and Dad decided to be with my sister, I wasn't going to let my plans get pushed to the side. We'd be staying home for Mother's Day.

Mother's Day arrived. In church that morning during the sermon, my mind wandered. Mom and Dad had spent so many holidays with me and few with my sister, so they'd decided to accept her invitation. I still stubbornly held my ground. My attention shifted back to the sermon as our pastor concluded his remarks with a story.

He told about a man who, while paying for a bouquet to send to his mother, noticed a tiny girl peeking through the window of the floral shop. As he opened the door, inviting her in, he congratulated himself for sending his mother flowers for Mother's Day. He knew he didn't have time to visit her; other matters needed his attention. "This was good enough," he reasoned.

Noticing that the girl was distraught, he asked her, "What's wrong?"

She meekly answered, "I only have one dollar, and the flowers I want for my mother cost two."

Immediately, he peeled a dollar bill from his money clip and handed it to her. She paid the cashier.

Then she asked if he would take her to her mother. Still feeling generous, he agreed. After a 10-minute drive, they came to the cemetery. There she asked to get out. He shut the car off and watched as this little girl walked a few steps and gently, lovingly placed her bouquet on her mother's freshly dug grave.

This same guy who had earlier ordered flowers for his mom returned to the floral shop as the owner was closing the door. He canceled his flower order and drove 200 miles to be with his mother on Mother's Day.

If my pastor said any more, I didn't hear it. I, like the son in the story, canceled my original plans and drove the hours so I too could be with both my mother and my sister on Mother's Day.

Prayer

Thank You, Lord Jesus, for mothers, especially my own. Forgive me for the times in my life when I've failed to honor her because I've stubbornly clung to my own agenda. Teach me who, not what, is ultimately important in my life. Thank You, Lord, for the way in which You honored Your mother, even as You were dying on the cross. Show me how to do the same. In Your holy name I pray. Amen.

Journal Jottings

Leave your journal unopened today. Use the time to ask forgiveness for when you neglected to be with your mother on a special day (birthday, Mother's Day, etc.).

Circle of Life

Now I know in part; then I shall know
fully, even as I am fully known.
1 Corinthians 13:12

As I listened to my nephew and his wife, along with their sponsors, make baptismal promises for their first child, I thought of when my husband and I, as sponsors, made the same promises for this nephew at his Baptism 28 years before. As the pastor pronounced the words, "I baptize you in the name of the Father, and of the Son, and of the Holy Spirit," I remembered watching as my nephew was sprinkled with the same water of grace.

How glad I was to witness the gift of forgiveness and eternal salvation to another generation. But it was difficult to accept how quickly time had passed. This day, more than others, reminded me of life's brevity. As I pondered our quick passing amidst the on-goingness of God, I recalled the prophet Isaiah's words. "All people are grass, their constancy is like the flowers of the field. ... The grass withers, the flower fades; but the Word of our God will stand forever" (Isaiah 40:6, 8 NRSV).

That morning, I stepped into the life of a person who was just beginning her earthly journey; by nightfall, I had stepped out of the life of a person whose journey on earth had ended.

Balloons shaped like butterflies, symbolic of resurrection and transformation, hung in the funeral parlor where my aunt's body lay. As I recognized the significance of the balloons—the shedding of my aunt's worn-out physical body to take on her new, glorious one—I reflected on this mysterious, miraculous circle of life and its deeper meaning.

What is this circle of life all about—this cycle from birth to death to resurrection? What happens when a Christian, like my aunt, dies? Why does God permit separation and such deep sadness to touch us? Will we ever know our loved ones again?

After reflecting on these questions, I asked one more. How can I feel such deep sadness and allow it to hinder me from experiencing the joy Christ intended for this journey?

As I stood near my aunt's casket, I was aware that I was not the only one who'd asked these unanswerable, larger-than-life questions. When facing these questions, I not only face a loved one's mortality, I face my own as well. I wonder what it will be like when my life has come full circle.

Left to my finite mind, I cannot comprehend the unanswerable. "Now we see but a poor reflection as in a mirror; then we shall see face to face. Now I know in part; then I shall know fully ..." (1 Corinthians 13:12 paraphrased).

Since my aunt's passing, I have come to realize, through Christ's gentle, but firm voice, the only way I can live with the unanswerable without becoming overwhelmed is to recognize that all these questions lead back to the Savior. The faith and hope I need so they don't overcome me remain in Him.

From Him alone, I must draw my strength. From Him alone, I must draw my trust. From Him alone, I must draw my hope. This hope will nourish me. This hope will keep unanswerable questions at bay. This thread of hope assures me that some day, in the fullness of time, all my questions will be answered. In His grace and the waters of Baptism, I walk sustained for the rest of my journey.

Prayer

Heavenly Father, though I see but in a mirror dimly, assure me that someday I'll fully comprehend the fulfillment of Your promises. As the unanswerable questions of life surround me, help me to draw my strength, trust, and hope from You. Through You, may these questions cease to hold their tenacious grip over me. In Your Son's name I pray. Amen.

Journal Jottings

What unanswerable questions trouble you? Note passages from God's Holy Word that help sustain you.

Unspoken Thoughts
WAITING FOR THE RIGHT MOMENT

The eyes of all look to You,
and You give them their food at the
proper time. Psalm 145:15

A friend had joined me for tea one afternoon a few days before my daughter's 17th birthday.

"So how's life going with you and your daughter now that she'll soon be ready for college?" my confidante asked while I poured our tea.

"Like it goes, I suppose, with any mother and daughter at this stage. She's trying to develop her own identity, cutting me off at times, and I'm trying to keep my cool when she does," I said.

We talked about the tensions between a mother and daughter during this weaning period. One day, they want to chat about everything. The next day, their tongues are caustic, preferring you not intrude on their turf.

"Do you suppose your daughter is trying to work through her adoption?" my friend asked.

I inhaled deeply, preferring not to talk about the subject. "If that's true, why hasn't she brought it up to me?" I said.

"Did you ever think she's afraid to, for fear you might brush her questions aside?" she carefully slipped in.

For a long time, we sat silent. Finally, I asked my friend if she thought there would ever be a "right moment" to talk with my daughter about her adoption. She said there would, but I would have to wait for it. "The eyes of all look to Thee, and Thou givest them their food in due season" (Psalm 145:15 RSV), she reassured me. She went on to say that God would give me the chance I needed to talk with my daughter about this delicate matter.

Taking my confidante's advice, I prayed, waited, and trusted God to show me the right moment.

Several weeks later, after school one day, my daughter bounced into the room where I was writing, ready to fill me in on the latest school happenings. When we reached the topic of homework, she said she had to write a poem about a life-shaping experience. I offered a few suggestions but to no avail. She didn't want her "writer Mom" composing her piece. I backed off. A while later I heard the computer starting up in her bedroom.

As I was putting my writing away for the night, my daughter skipped in and asked if I'd check her rough draft for grammatical mistakes only. When I read the title, "Tragedy of my Baby Mom," my mouth dropped. She'd written about the two moms of her life—one she'd never met.

After tweaking her poem for grammar errors, we sat on the sofa and opened up to each another. Candidly, we shared thoughts that up to this day we'd left unspoken for fear we might hurt the other's feelings.

In that poem and the conversation that ensued, a daughter's pent-up emotions and a mother's guarded feelings were finally spoken. Christ had made the right moment so.

Prayer

Lord God, thank You for giving me courage and strength when I'm reluctant to approach my daughter with a sensitive subject. Remind me to always look to You for guidance. Send Your Holy Spirit to empower me to pray, wait, and trust You to give me the time and the words I need. And help me make the most of each opportunity I have to witness to Your faithfulness to me. In Your Son's saving name I pray. Amen.

Journal Jottings

Is there a topic you and a loved one need to talk about? Describe it here, then ask God to show you the right moment.

Missed Exit

And having been warned in a dream
not to go back ... they returned to their
country by another route. Matthew 2:12

During our three-hour road trip from Williamsburg, Virginia, to Washington, D.C., that August morning, our family spent our traveling time outlining an itinerary for the days we'd spend in the nation's capital. Rather than driving into the heart of the city that first day, we planned to stay on the outskirts and tour Arlington National Cemetery. The next day, we'd board the Metro (subway) to downtown to the Washington Mall and tour the monuments and United States Capitol. After we saw how our first two days unfolded, we'd plan our final ones. We knew, along with several Smithsonian Museums, we wanted to see the Holocaust Museum and perhaps the White House.

As the cityscape of Washington, D.C., glimmered in the hazy noon sky and we were crunched in six lanes of busy traffic, we looked for the brown sign directing us to the national cemetery. When our daughter spotted it, the sign indicated we'd be turning left in one-half mile. Quickly, we moved into the lane closest to us turning left.

As it turned out, due to street construction, the lane we were in did not exit to Arlington National Cemetery. Frustrated and perplexed, we cruised by our intended destination, eventually ending up in the heart of the city, near the monuments and capitol building.

In the midst of the commotion and confusion of having missed our turn and gotten on another route, I thought of the Wise Men and how, through a dream, God pointed them in a different direction than they had planned. His direction protected both baby Jesus and them from King Herod (Matthew 2:1–12), so His plan for Jesus' life, death, and resurrection would be fulfilled in due time.

Clearly, we hadn't been warned by God in a dream that we should alter our route. Nevertheless, after we missed our turn, we were unable to correct our situation. Street construction was everywhere. Now we'd ended up in downtown Washington D.C., exactly where we'd intended to be the next day.

I wondered, *might God be trying to point us in a different direction? Might He be asking us to flip-flop our days, to see the city by taking a route other than the one we had planned?*

When I shared my thoughts with my husband and daughter, they agreed with me. Rather than fighting our way back to Arlington National Cemetery in the horrendous traffic, we decided to tour the capitol and monuments while we were in the vicinity. We'd save the national cemetery for the next day.

That evening we watched the local news. The reporter was in the Washington Mall area announcing late breaking developments. "Tomorrow, at 9:00 a.m., a white supremacy group is scheduled to march from the Washington Monument to the United States Capitol. Massive numbers of counter-demonstrators are expected to rally against the group. Several hundred police are assigned to the area to ensure that no violent confrontations take place. We'll have the latest update on tomorrow's morning news."

My heart skipped a beat. My family would have been touring this same area at the same time as the march was planned. I was overcome with thanks.

Prayer

Father God, I know that the guidance You gave the Wise Men was part of Your perfect plan for our salvation. Show me how Your guidance in my life is part of Your plan to lead me to reunion with You in heaven. Guide me to trust Your gracious guiding hand. In Your name I pray. Amen.

Journal Jottings

Describe a time when you felt the Holy Spirit move you to change your plans to protect you.

Watching a Day Unfold

UNIMPEDED BY AN AGENDA

For You make me glad by Your deeds,
O LORD. Psalm 92:4

We'd spent several days in Williamsburg, Virginia, and Washington, D.C., on a tight schedule so we could see as many of the landmarks and historic sites as we could. Now, unlike the previous, memorable days dictated by an agenda, we could allow these next few days visiting friends in Duck, North Carolina, to unfold as freely and naturally as they would. There was no agenda, no schedule that I had created for us to follow.

My husband and I started out that morning not having a clue where the day would take us or what experiences would unfold. After driving down the coast road along the Outer Banks, we saw the sign pointing to Kitty Hawk. We stopped for a while at the memorial and museum built in honor of these aviation pioneers, admiring their fortitude and courage with which they ushered in the age of manned flight.

Four miles down the road, we were amazed to come upon Jockey's Ridge, a 40-acre tract of fine sand deposited by the coastal winds with dunes climbing as high as 100 feet. We gazed with astonishment as colorful hang gliders took flight from the peaks of the dunes.

Driving another few miles down the scenic path, we came to the inlet. There, near the end of the day, we discovered charter boats hauling in their catch of fish. Pushing my wheelchair down the wet, wooden planks of the boardwalk, with the smell of fresh fish penetrating the air, we were soon caught up by the crowd moving from one fishing boat to another. We gawked as the deckhands threw their day's catch onto the boardwalk, enticing the tourists.

Stopping by the last moored fishing boat, we saw the armfuls of fish the crew tossed onto the dock. The party who had chartered this boat for the day had caught more fish than their cooler could hold. We heard them offering their remaining fish, all mahi mahi, to the captain, a small wrinkled man dressed in soiled khaki shorts and a sea-stained T-shirt bearing the boat's name, "Dream Girl."

Captivated by the speed and dexterity with which the deckhand sliced the fish open, I moved my wheelchair through the crowd to snap his picture. Glistening with perspiration, he grinned at me broadly then resumed his task.

After we watched the deckhand fillet his last mahi mahi, my husband grabbed my wheelchair to push me back up the boardwalk. From behind my chair, I heard a voice say, "Here, have some mahi mahi."

Before I could respond, a plastic bag of fillets, weighing approximately two pounds, landed in my lap. Wishing to express my thankfulness, I looked back. All I could see was the man walking away. No longer could he hear me.

We carefully packed our "catch" in an ice chest we had in our car. Back at the condo, we baked it and served the mahi mahi as a delectable appetizer, to the raves of all.

In our bedroom that night, as I looked out the window to the vast ocean horizon, I thought about the unexpected blessings of this day and recognized the subtle lesson Christ had taught me. I can't plan for or schedule these blessings in my life: the beauty of God's natural world, the generosity of a total stranger, and the complete forgiveness of my transgressions in Christ. I can simply receive them as gifts from God. "O Lord, You make me glad by Your deeds" (Psalm 92:4, paraphrased).

Prayer

Heavenly Father, giver of all life's blessings, thank You for imparting to me Your kindest, simplest blessings. Help me to focus on You rather than on agendas and schedules. Keep me rooted in Your Word and renewed in the gifts of Your grace. Thank You for reconciling me to You in Your Son. In His name I pray. Amen.

Journal Jottings

Create a day when you aren't restricted by an agenda or activity-driven schedule. Tell what you discover.

All of These Shoes

For we brought nothing into the world,
and we can take nothing out of it.
1 Timothy 6:7

Initially, what drew me to Lila was her bubbling enthusiasm. She was dressed in a classy red suit that complemented her energetic spirit. We met only once, and in the course of our brief conversation I asked, "When you switched to your newer, lighter-weight leg braces, could you still wear your old shoes?"

"Of course not," she said. "They weren't wide enough."

Then I asked the question that had really been troubling me. "What did you do with your old shoes?"

Without a moment's hesitation, she quipped, "I boxed them up and took them to my favorite charity."

That night, after I'd gotten home from our support group meeting, I opened my closet full of shoes. *How could Lila part with her shoes all at once?* I wondered. As attached as I was to my shoes, I couldn't imagine that I'd ever have that kind of resolve.

Each pair of shoes on my closet shelf told a story all their own—starting with the person who'd helped me pick them out, to Steve, my compassionate repairman who'd rebuilt them so I could stand straight. Although I sensed what Lila had done was better than any plan I could come up with, it was just too hard for me to part with all those shoes, especially all at one time.

I devised a trade-off. When I wanted to wear my newer, lighter-weight braces, most likely for everyday, I'd wear wider-width shoes, although I thought they were less attractive. For dressier occasions, I would wear my old narrow-width shoes, which were much prettier, and my older, heavier braces. To my chagrin, however, switching braces and shoes back and forth caused my back to become unbearably sore and fatigued.

Still without a solution that appeased me, I spotted a sun catcher in a gift catalog that read "Don't Look Back." The sun catcher featured a child just having crossed an intersection. At the intersection were two signs. One pointed backward and read "No Longer an Option." The other sign pointed forward and read "Your Life." The child had obviously followed the sign pointed forward and was happily moving in that direction, knapsack slung over her shoulder.

I'll bet that's one of Lila's secrets too, I mused. *She never looks back.*

I told myself the same could be true of me. I could trade in that bag of stuff I've accumulated—those shoes I could no longer wear—for a much lighter knapsack—fewer shoes. I could move forward with anticipation, no longer burdened by my attachment to the past.

As I move forward with other things in my life, I'm learning to discard more and accumulate less. As the apostle Paul wrote to Timothy years ago, so he instructs me today, "We brought nothing into the world, and we can take nothing out of it" (1 Timothy 6:7). True happiness is not based on our accumulated possessions. It comes from being connected to the Giver of all good things—the Source of all joy. It becomes real as we receive Christ through Word and Sacrament. And it is manifested in the many ways we can serve others in His name. The joy we receive from leading a faithful life leads to greater fullness than any amount of material goods.

I ordered the sun catcher. Then I hauled in a big card-board box, tossed in my old shoes, gave them to charity—and never looked back.

Prayer

O God, enable me to look to the future, not back to what once was. As You remind me through the apostle Paul, "We brought nothing into this world, and we can take nothing out of it" (1 Timothy 6:7). Teach me to rejoice in the blessings in my life and to seek Your kingdom above all other things. In Jesus' name. Amen.

Journal Jottings

What part of your past could you shed so you are better able to move forward?

Without the Rain

IF THE SUN ALWAYS SHINES

"A tree is recognized by its fruit."
Matthew 12:33

My mother and I inched our way through the sea of mothers and daughters at the banquet to thank the guest speaker for her entertaining, provocative message. What did she do when my mother and I reached her, but weave yet another story.

A farmer planned an experiment to test the effect of sunlight and rain on apple trees. He divided the trees into two equal groups. The first group of trees he grew under normal conditions, allowing both sunshine and rain to fall upon them. He raised the second group in a controlled environment, permitting sunshine but no rainfall. When it was harvest time, the apple trees that had received only sunshine bore no fruit. The trees grown in both sunlight and rain, however, produced plump, juicy apples.

The speaker smiled, "We think how nice it would be if rain never fell on our lives." With a quick hug, she thanked us for putting up with her unending stories.

That night, I thought about the Bible story of the Samaritan woman at the well (John 4:1–30, 39–42). I thought, *if rain had not fallen on the life of this woman, if there had been only sunny days for her, would she have been as receptive to Jesus' offer of living water?*

When our Savior anticipated the pain and suffering of His crucifixion, He begged His Father to take it from Him. But He knew the only way to fulfill God's plan of salvation was to endure unimaginable agony for our sins. Without the pain of our sin, His death and resurrection would be meaningless.

The question came closer to home. If rain hadn't fallen on me, if my life had always been sunny and happy, would I understand how Christ is transforming me? Where would I be were it not for the dark days in my life? This question led me to compose this poem.

Without the Rain

Without the rain,
I wouldn't savor life's ordinary moments nearly as much.

Without the rain,
I couldn't comprehend the pain
of permanently saying good-bye to my love,
the ecstasy, a year later,
of feeling my love's returning embrace.

Without the rain,
I wouldn't realize the strength and shelter
a family provides.

Without the rain,
I couldn't fathom how a sister's miscarriage
could bond two sisters' hearts forever.

Without the rain,
I might not discern which relationships to keep,
and which to let drift away.

Without the rain,
I would never have perceived what it means
to have a daughter born "from my heart, not in it."

Without the rain,
I couldn't sympathize with others who have experienced
the frustrating feeling of joblessness.

Without the rain,
I wouldn't understand how a person can become
"better, not bitter."

Without the rain,
I could never imagine the empathy and compassion
people sharing the same kind of suffering
can extend to one another.

Without the rain,
I wouldn't have discovered
who my true friends are.

Without the rain,
I would never know
what it means to pray all night for a mother I hold dear.

Without the rain,
I couldn't grasp
a counselor's quiet understanding.

Without the rain,
I could never have glimpsed
the bleak reality of death,
the birthing into eternal life.

Without the rain,
it might have been harder for me to recognize
the Source of my true strength.

Without the rain,
I might not have emerged the empowered,
fruit-filled woman
Christ is helping me become ...

So how important is the rain to my life? I ask myself again. Vital to my tree's final fruit.

Prayer

Remind me, heavenly Father, when I desire only the sunshine—the easy, smooth path through life—that it also takes the rain to help me understand the woman You transform me to be, blessed and fruit-filled. Growing, because of You. Keep my eyes on the cross so I might remember the agony of Jesus' death for my sins and anticipate the blessings of eternal life. In Jesus' name. Amen.

Journal Jottings

Describe how Christ shaped and transformed your life from the rains that have fallen on it.

Beginnings Revisited
DOUBTING GOD

*You open Your hand and satisfy
the desires of every living thing.
Psalm 145:16*

How could I pull this mass of scattered, confusing, incongruent thoughts from my journal—thoughts between God and me—into a meaningful book? Although I wanted to, I strongly doubted I could. How could these seeds of thought grow into anything?

With these doubts plaguing me, I attended a writers' conference. There, God in His gentle yet definitive voice made it clear He wanted me to write a book about the everyday obstacles I'd overcome through His power in my life.

What I had to offer God seemed to be almost nothing— a few disjointed journals and Christmas letters. The little I knew about writing, I'd picked up either in my college English classes, through my brief teaching career, or at a smidgen of writers' conferences. Even so, God promised to show me everything I needed to construct my book. If I'd put in the tough work of grinding out these stories—these threads of hope—listening for His voice in them, He'd provide the rest. I felt inadequate for the task He was calling me to do, but the words from a plaque I saw at the writers' conference kept urging me forward. "You open Your hand and satisfy the desires of every living thing" (Psalm 145:16).

God had promised He'd provide me with everything I needed. Everything. So why was I doubtful? I couldn't get a grip on this question, until I revisited the stories of Abraham, Moses, and Mary Magdalene; stories I'd reflected on earlier when exploring the "How Can I?" question. This time, I wanted an answer to another question. "Did God really provide these people with everything they needed, as He'd promised?"

I considered Abraham. Under the stars that night, God told the childless Abraham that he would become the "father of nations," and God provided. Although Sarah had passed the change in her life and was much too old to bear a child, God brought her into a state of child-bearing (Genesis 17:1–8; 18:1–15; 21:1–8).

When God told Moses to lead the Israelites out of Egypt to the Promised Land, he strongly questioned whether he could. It was a huge logistical undertaking to lead hundreds of thousands of people and provide food and shelter for them for an indefinite time. God sent Moses' brother Aaron to be his spokesperson (Exodus 4:10–17). In addition, God dispensed all the daily provisions the Israelites needed the whole time they were in the wilderness, manifesting these in manna, quail, and springs of water (Exodus 15:22–25, 27; 16:13–18).

I wondered if Mary Magdalene had doubts after Jesus cast out her seven demons (Mark 16:9) and she joined Him in Galilee (Matthew 27:55–56). During her journey with Him, though, Christ provided her with confidence, an assurance she would need to announce His resurrection (John 20:11–18). As God had promised, He'd delivered.

Would God provide for me in the same way when I wrote my book? The question lingered. All I could do was refocus on His Word, feast at His Table, pray hard, put my confidence in Him every step of the way, and get to work as He directed.

From the book's onset, God provided me with a publishing company receptive to the same vision. I soon realized this book would have to be formatted on a computer. My sister's forte was operating computers. She taught me the ins and outs of computer management, all the way from purchasing to operating one.

When I got into the thick of writing, it became apparent I didn't have the strength and energy needed to write and prepare nutritious meals for my family every day. My daughter and husband efficiently took over, so much so, they think I've forgotten how to cook. As I moved midway into creating this book, I sensed I'd need more material than what I could glean from my journal and Christmas letters. New faces and voices appeared, bringing me new experiences and fresh ideas from which to write.

From conception to mid-point to completion, God has opened His hand and provided me with everything I need. I have felt His strong presence, encouraging, growing, and affirming this project. The God who gave me this task several years ago miraculously has given me the provisions to accomplish it, each step of the way.

Does God provide? Can mere seeds, placed in His hand, spring forth and become much more? This book attests to God's unequivocal yes.

Prayer

Heavenly Father, sometimes my faith is weak, my mind fills with doubt. Forgive my sin of doubt. Strengthen my faith, Lord, and show me how to trust and put complete confidence in You. Keep me ever mindful that You provide for me and guide my journey every step of the way, just like You did for Your servants Abraham, Moses, and Mary Magdalene. For "You open Your hand and satisfy our desires," lavishing upon me Your amazing gifts. Oh, Lord, how marvelous are Your ways. To You alone be the glory! In Jesus' name. Amen.

Journal Jottings

Write about a time when you doubted God's promise to provide for your needs, and He gave you everything you needed.

No Longer Ugly

OVERCOMING A DEVASTATED IMAGE

*The Spirit of the LORD will come upon you
in power ... and you will be changed into
a different person. 1 Samuel 10:6*

There was a time in my life when I was facing a roller coaster of emotions, feeling ugly, hopeless, unfulfilled. Christ used my mother and father, my Christian giants, along with my supportive daughter and husband, to hold me up. Had it not been for my mother's tenacious love during that time, I shudder to think what might have happened to me. Every day, she called or visited. Those chats helped sustain me. They gave me strength and faith to get through another day. Christ sent other people to guide and support me through this challenging time.

Although I've never understood why Christ allowed me to stumble over such large hurdles, I've held, as firmly as I could, to a Bible verse my mother often quoted. "We know that in everything God works for good with those who love Him, who are called according to His purpose" (Romans 8:28 RSV).

I cannot say exactly how it happened. I only know it did. Christ changed me from seeing myself as an ugly, hopeless, incapable person—an "ugly bird"—to seeing myself as a confident, hope-filled, competent woman.

I first sensed it the night I stood next to my mother's seemingly lifeless body as she lay in intensive care. Christ enfolded me with His loving presence. In that moment I realized, through His power, that the same strong faith, the same tenacious strength, and the same resilient spirit embodied in my mother lived also in me.

As Christ has helped me across my hurdles since then, I've learned some other important truths.

Christ has shown me how to be less rigid with life, to relinquish control and allow my life to flow as God has planned it, not as I think it should. If I had not contracted polio, life wouldn't necessarily have been better; it only would have been different. God is often a God of reversals. He can take my physical weakness, with all its loss, grief, anger, and pain, and unearth from it a blessing. This blessing can in turn be used to help others who are hurting.

I learned that external beauty is fleeting and unimportant. Knowing who I am and Whose I am is far greater than external splendor. If I am aware of who I am and to Whom I belong, I won't be frustrated by trying to be someone I am not. Christ made me unique, to serve a definite purpose in His kingdom on earth. He's given me a voice. My voice counts. I need only listen and trust the voice and instincts He's given me. He's made clear what I need to take from life. Even more important, He's revealed what I need to give back to Him.

Although Christ has taught me much, I've more to learn before I'm truly able to grasp the thread of hope that is present in every situation, to see His face in everything I encounter. Through the Holy Spirit's power, I'm on my way to becoming the woman God intends me to be. I recognize there's an incompleteness to this life, one that will be finished only when I am blessed with my glorified body.

One of the most beautiful things spoken to me came when I was almost finished with this book. With tenderness, my dad said, "I can't believe the change that has taken place in you as you've been writing."

Mom affirmed his words, "Yes, she's become a woman."

These words brought tears and confirmed what I had been feeling. I was no longer the "ugly bird." Christ has transformed me from seeing myself as a devastated person to seeing that I am restored, empowered, and complete in Him.

When I started writing this book, I thought I was the only woman who felt incomplete, lonely, and hopeless. Since then I've discovered I am not alone in these feelings or this journey.

Christ began His work in me at Baptism, and every day continues to move my life forward into a splendid mystery, one only He could have planned. He continuously shapes and redesigns me. Like Mary Magdalene, I know "the Spirit of the Lord has come upon me in power and has changed me into a different person" (1 Samuel 10:6, paraphrased).

For Mary Magdalene, it meant announcing the Lord's resurrection. For me, the purpose and the call are just beginning to unfold, like a flower in the morning sun, petal by delicate petal. I don't know where Christ will lead me, but I know that He wants me to share my own experiences to encourage others in their faith walk with Him. And I know that through this writing, God has bestowed amazing gifts, gifts that started with simple threads of thought. Through these threads God has opened a new purpose and fulfillment for my life. Though I will at times backslide, yet like Mary Magdalene, I walk forward—hopeful, confident, and unafraid.

Prayer

Thank You, Heavenly Father, for taking my ugly self-image and making it new. Through You, I share in the victory—empowered and complete in my Baptism. Make me worthy of Your promise, and guide all I say and do so I will glorify You throughout my life. I praise Your lasting name. In Jesus' name I pray. Amen.

Journal Jottings

Describe how has Christ taken your ugly self-image and changed it so you see yourself as renewed in Him.